The SHEPHERD
AS
PREACHER

John MacArthur
GENERAL EDITOR

HARVEST HOUSE PUBLISHERS
EUGENE, OREGON

THE SHEPHERD AS PREACHER

Copyright © 2015 Grace Community Church
Published by Harvest House Publishers
Eugene, Oregon 97402
www.harvesthousepublishers.com

ISBN 978-0-7369-6207-0 (pbk.)
ISBN 978-0-7369-6208-7 (eBook)

Library of Congress Cataloging-in-Publication Data
    The shepherd as preacher / John MacArthur, general editor.
        pages cm. — (The shepherd's library) 1. Preaching—Congresses. I. MacArthur, John, 1939- editor.
    BV4202.S54 2015
    251—dc23

                                                                    2014028524

Printed in the United States of America

            15 16 17 18 19 20 21 22 23 / LB-JH / 10 9 8 7 6 5 4 3 2 1

CONTENTS

INTRODUCTION

The first Shepherds' Conference was held on March 19, 1980, at Grace Community Church, where 159 men gathered to focus on the theme of pastoral ministry. From the beginning, the goal was to live out Paul's mandate to Timothy: "The things which you have heard from me in the presence of many witnesses, entrust these to faithful men who will be able to teach others also" (2 Timothy 2:2).

What started as a small event has, by God's grace, blossomed into an international movement with thousands in attendance each spring. Over the years, pastors from every state and nearly 100 countries have come to the conference to be challenged and encouraged in areas of preaching, theology, leadership, discipleship, and counseling. My own heart has been deeply blessed by the faithful men I've met and fellowshipped with at the conference.

Since its inception, the Shepherds' Conference has featured hundreds of sermons specifically directed at pastors and church leaders. Because the truth of God's Word is timeless, those messages are still as rich and powerful today as when they were first preached. That is why I was so thrilled when Harvest House Publishers approached me about publishing this volume—a collection of the most memorable Shepherds' Conference messages on the topic of preaching. Nothing is more urgently needed in today's church than the faithful proclamation of God's Word, which is why a book on this subject is so timely. In keeping with Paul's instruction to Timothy, the aim of this volume is to encourage pastors to fulfill their pastoral mandate: to preach the Word in season and out of season (2 Timothy 4:2). The chapters that follow have been edited as minimally as possible so that they reflect the original content of the Shepherd's Conference messages.

This book is for all who preach and teach the Scriptures, whether they have been to the Shepherds' Conference or not. As you read it, my prayer is that your passion for truth will burn brighter and your resolve for Christ's glory will grow stronger as you seek to serve His church through the faithful exposition of His Word.

For the Great Shepherd,
John MacArthur

PREACH THE WORD

"Preach the word; be ready in season and out of season,
reprove, rebuke, exhort with great
patience and instruction."

2 TIMOTHY 4:2

1

PREACH THE WORD

John MacArthur
Shepherds' Conference 1998

2 Timothy 3:1–4:4

There is a text of Scripture that is beloved by me, and one upon which I have preached numerous times through the years. It is a text that my father wrote inside the flyleaf of a Bible that he gave to me when I told him I felt called to preach. The text is 2 Timothy 4:2: "Preach the word; be ready in season and out of season, reprove, rebuke, exhort with great patience and instruction."

That brief verse defines biblical ministry in one central command: "Preach the Word." Along with this command you could add 1 Timothy 3:2, which says pastors, overseers, and elders are to be skilled in teaching and preaching. We are to preach the Word skillfully. That is our calling, and this verse is definitive because it speaks so concisely, calling us to "preach the Word."

Now you will notice that the apostle Paul addresses the time and the tone of our preaching. The time is "in season and out of season." We could debate what that means, but if I can lead you to a simple conclusion, the only possibilities are to be in season or out of season; therefore, it means all the time. We are to preach the Word all the time. There is no time when we change that commission, no time when that method of ministry is set aside for something else. Preaching the Word is to be done all the time.

As for the tone, it is twofold: There is the negative aspect of reproving and rebuking, and there is the positive aspect of taking God's truth and exhorting people with great patience and instruction. Negatively we are to confront error and sin. Positively we are to teach sound doctrine and godly living. We are to exhort people to be obedient to the Word, and we are to have great patience and allow them the time to mature in their obedience.

**If every word of God is true and pure,
and every word is food for the believer,
then every word is to be proclaimed.**

This is a simple command: Preach the Word all the time. Jesus said, "Man shall not live on bread alone, but on every word that proceeds out of the mouth of God" (Matthew 4:4). That truth calls us to an expository ministry in which we deal with every word that proceeds out of the mouth of God. If every word of God is true and pure, and every word is food for the believer, then every word is to be proclaimed.

People are starving for God's Word but they don't know it. They are hungry, they are reaching out, they are grasping. They realize the hollow places in their life, the shallowness, the lack of insight, the lack of understanding. They cannot solve the problems of life. They are starving for God's Word and are being offered substitutes that do not help. God has ordained that His Word be brought to them because it alone can feed them, and the delivery method is preaching. Paul wrote, "How will they hear without a preacher?" (Romans 10:14). Martin Luther said, "The highest worship of God is the preaching of the Word."[1] God is revealed through His Word; therefore, preaching His Word is preaching His character, His will, and all that defines Him in true terms and exalts Him as He is to be exalted.

Our mandate then comes not from the culture, it comes from heaven. It is the God of heaven who has mandated us through the pages of Scripture to preach the Word, to preach every word, and to bring to starving souls the only food that feeds—the truth of God. The Bible is the inerrant and infallible Word of the living God. It is sharper than any two-edged sword, and every word in it is pure and true. We are to preach God's Word in its entirety and to unfold all its truth. That is the command.

This concise, clear, and unequivocal command to preach the Word is supported by five potent realities that motivate us in this endeavor. Even though these five realities are potent enough individually to motivate a man to preach the Word of God, together they provide a formidable set of motivations like no other text of Scripture.

Preach the Word Because of the Danger of the Seasons (3:1-9)

First, we are to preach the Word because of the danger of the seasons. In 2 Timothy 3:1 Paul prefaced his instruction by telling Timothy, "Realize this, that in the last days…" The last days began when the Messiah came the first time. The apostle John said, "Children, it is the last hour" (1 John 2:18). Paul wrote, "…in the last days difficult times will come" (2 Timothy 3:1). The phrase "difficult times" can be translated "seasons" rather than "times." It is not a reference to clock time or calendar time. The word used here in the original Greek text is *kairos*, which means seasons, epochs, or movements. The word translated "difficult" could have been translated "dangerous," or even "savage." Dangerous, perilous times will come. These times will threaten the truth, the gospel, and the church. According to 2 Timothy 3:13, they will increase in severity because "evil men and impostors will proceed from bad to worse, deceiving and being deceived." From the beginning of the last days until Jesus comes, there will be an escalating severity and frequency of these dangerous epochs.

We are talking about movements and epochs that began when Jesus came and started the church, and they have continued cumulatively. They do not come and go; rather, they come and stay, and increase in frequency, so that there is greater danger now than there has ever been. These epochs define for us the danger that threatens the life of the church and the truth. Let's look at some of them, suggested by J.W. Montgomery in his book *Damned Through the Church*.[2]

The Dangerous Epochs
Sacramentalism

The first and most prominent epoch of danger thrust upon the church began in the fourth century—sacramentalism. This began with the development of the Holy Roman Empire and Constantine, which blossomed into the Roman Catholic system of salvation by ritual. The church became a surrogate Christ—that is, people were connected to the church and to the system rather than to Christ through a personal relationship with Him. Sacramentalism became the enemy of the true gospel, the enemy of grace and faith, and led to the persecution and execution of true believers. It was not until the Reformation in the sixteenth century that sacramentalism began to weaken.

Rationalism

Not long after the Reformation came the second epoch of danger—rationalism. As people came out of the Reformation and entered the Renaissance and Industrial Revolution, they broke away from the monolithic institution of Roman Catholicism and got their own identity back and began to think for themselves. They began to discover, invent, and develop things and feel their freedom. They began to worship their own minds, and human reason became god. Thomas Paine wrote *The Age of Reason*, in which he debunked the Bible and affirmed that the human mind is god, and the Bible became a slave to rationalism. Rationalists assaulted Scripture and denied its miracles, its inspiration, the deity of Christ, and the gospel of grace—all in the name of scholarship and human reason.

These epochs have not disappeared. We still have sacramental religions all around the world, and we still have rationalism. Rationalism has destroyed every seminary in Europe. I will never forget visiting St. Salvator's Chapel at the University of St. Andrews in Scotland and standing in the pulpit where John Knox launched the Scottish Reformation. At a time when Rome was in power, John Knox came and preached the gospel of grace and faith in the midst of a works-based system. He took his stand against this massive and powerful system that held people in religious bondage.

Outside that little chapel, on one of the cobblestone streets nearby, there are three sets of initials. These initials represent the names of three young students who, in their late teens, heard the preaching of John Knox, believed the gospel, and turned to Jesus Christ by faith. Consequently, they were burned at the stake by the Catholic authorities. As a tribute to these students, their initials were inscribed on the street at the spot where they were burned. Right across the street is the theological college at the University of St. Andrews. Every day, the faculty of that school walks to the pub across the street, stepping on the initials of the martyrs who died for the truth that these rationalist theologians reject. They worship the god of human intellect and deny the veracity of Scripture.

Orthodoxism

Rationalism was followed by orthodoxism—a cold, dead, and indifferent orthodoxy. Although in the nineteenth century huge strides in printing technology allowed for mass production of Bibles, many people were indifferent to it because their orthodoxy was dead and cold. Their spirituality was either shallow or nonexistent.

Politicism

Then came politicism. The church became preoccupied with gaining political power. It developed the social gospel, reconstruction, and liberation theology all in an attempt to bring change through human means rather than through salvation in Christ.

Ecumenism

Ecumenism was the fifth dangerous epoch, and it erupted during the 1950s. Everyone was talking about unity and setting aside dogma to prevent divisions over doctrinal issues. This produced sentimentalism, and along came a new hermeneutic for interpreting Scripture called "the Jesus Ethic." Jesus was defined as a nice guy who would have never said anything harsh, so the proponents of ecumenism took judgment and retribution out of the Bible. Evil was tolerated and doctrine was disdained, which led to a lack of discernment.

Experientialism

The sixth epoch was experientialism, which characterized the 1960s. Truth was defined as a feeling that originated in intuition, visions, prophecies, or special revelations. One no longer looked to the objective Word of God to determine truth, but rather, to some subjective intuition. This perspective posed an immense danger to the church and drew people away from the Word of God.

Subjectivism

The seventh epoch was subjectivism. In the 1980s, psychology captured the church and many believers got into narcissistic navel gazing. They were concerned about whether they could bump themselves up the comfort ladder a little bit and become more successful and make more money. They developed man-centered and needs-based theology. As a result, personal comfort became the ultimate goal.

Mysticism

Mysticism was the eighth epoch, developing in the 1990s and permitting people to believe in whatever they wanted. Concurrently, pragmatism allowed people to define ministry. The church was said to exist to serve people. A minister determined his plan of ministry by distributing a survey to find out what people wanted. Truth became the servant of what works. Expository preaching was viewed as a pony-express method of delivery in a computer age to a lot of folks who did not want it in the first place. The key to effective ministry was said to be image or style rather than content.

Syncretism

The ninth epoch was syncretism—the belief that all monotheistic religions worship the same God, and all monotheists are going to heaven. Our culture likes to suppose that heaven will be occupied by followers of Confucius, Buddha, Mohammed, orthodox Jews, and even atheists because they all sought the truth. That's syncretism.

As you can see, the church has faced one dangerous epoch after another and they never go away. Rather, they stay and accumulate so that the church is dealing with all of them. As a shepherd, you are facing a formidable set of fortresses (2 Corinthians 10:4-5). They are strong and well-designed ideological fortifications that must be countered skillfully with God's truth. This requires that you be effective in your handling of the Word. It is not easy to be discerning, to understand the issues that face us, and to bring the appropriate portion of Scripture to bear upon the imminent dangers all around us. Most of Christianity does not care, but we who bear the responsibility as shepherds of God's flock do. These dangers are accumulating and worsening, resulting in a lack of discernment and a growing disdain for doctrine.

The Guilty and the Gullible

Starting in 2 Timothy 3:2, Paul further defines these dangerous seasons by describing the people who are behind them. They are "lovers of self, lovers of money, boastful, arrogant, revilers, disobedient to parents, ungrateful, unholy, unloving, irreconcilable, malicious gossips, without self-control, brutal, haters of good, treacherous, reckless, conceited, lovers of pleasure rather than lovers of God" (3:2-4). Now if you applied that list to anyone today, would it not be politically incorrect? Can you imagine someone confronting another individual in error and going through that list? It reminds me of Jesus' approach. He went up to the religious leaders of His day who were in error and said, "You snakes, you vipers, you dogs, you filthy, stinking, wretched tombs painted white." How well would that work today?

In 2 Timothy 3:5, Paul reveals that false teachers have a form of godliness. The face that they want to portray is of godliness, but power is absent. They do not have the power of God because they do not know God. Second Timothy 3:6 goes on to say they "enter into households and captivate weak women weighed down with sins, led on by various impulses." Today they enter homes through the media as well as in person, and they target women, whom God designed to be protected by faithful men. They captivate weak women who are weighed down with sins and teach them error. Just like Jannes and Jambres, the two magicians in Egypt who opposed Moses, these men oppose the truth. These false teachers have depraved minds, and they should be rejected.

We need godly men who can go into the fray, men who understand the Word of God clearly. Satan's deceptions are not without subtlety. It is not always obvious on the surface what is actually going on. That's why we need formidable men who understand God's Word. We need men who understand the issues of their time, who have a holy courage, and who are willing to step into the battle so they can assault the enemy graciously and relentlessly with the truth.

In 2 Corinthians 10:4, Paul says our job as shepherds is to smash ideological fortresses and bring everyone who is captive into obedience to Christ. We want to set free those who are held captive in the fortresses that these dangerous epochs have erected. We are called to guard the truth and preach the truth. We cannot do either if we do not understand the truth. It takes well-trained men to stand against the subtleties and nuances of Satan's devices.

Preach the Word Because of the Devotion of the Saints *(3:10-14)*

The second reason we must preach the Word is because of the devotion of the saints. In 2 Timothy 3:10-11, Paul charged Timothy, "Now you followed my teaching, conduct, purpose, faith, patience, love, perseverance, persecutions, and sufferings." In other words, "Timothy, you followed me, you were my disciple and I went through the patterns of ministry for you. You saw my purpose and my ministry duty—teaching and living—so proclaim and live the truth in Jesus' name. You saw how I taught it and I lived it; that is my integrity." Paul was relentlessly focused on the responsibility he had to proclaim the truth. And Timothy saw Paul's faithfulness to this purpose. He persevered in his love for people and God even in the face of persecution and suffering.

In summary, Paul said, "You saw how I ministered. You saw the way I did it. I did it with love. I did it with focus. I did it relentlessly. I did it patiently. I did it lovingly. I took the flack. I took the pain. I took the suffering. I took the imprisonments. I took the beatings, the whippings, and the stonings. You were with me at Antioch, Iconium, and Lystra; you saw all that."

Paul then challenged Timothy to "continue in the things you have learned and become convinced of, knowing from whom you have learned them" (2 Timothy 3:14). He said, "Timothy, you just do exactly what I told you to do." Many people today want to reinvent ministry, have you noticed? But Paul said, "Do it exactly the way I told you to do it."

In 2 Timothy 3:17 Paul went on to call Timothy the "man of God." That is a technical term used only twice in the New Testament, both times in Timothy. It is used over 70 times in the Old Testament, and every time it refers to a preacher. Paul was saying, "Timothy, you are just another man of God. There is a long line of these men of God—men called by God and gifted by Him to proclaim His truth. You cannot get out of step. You cannot go your way or invent your own approach. You are one man in a long line of men who are called to preach the Word. That is what you are to do."

That is how I look at my own life, and it brings to mind a childhood memory about my grandfather. He was a faithful preacher of the Word of God all through his ministry right up until his death. While he was on his deathbed at home, my father and I were there, and my father asked him, "Dad, is there anything you want?" My grandfather responded, "Yes, I want to preach one more time." While dying from cancer, he wanted just one thing: to preach one more time. He had prepared a sermon he had not preached. That is hard for a preacher to handle; that is fire in his bones. He needs to get it out.

My grandfather had prepared a sermon on heaven and died without ever being able to preach it. So my dad took his notes, printed them, and passed them out to everybody at the funeral. In that way, my grandfather preached on heaven from heaven. That incident had a tremendous effect on me as a young boy. What a faithful man—right down to the last breath, all my grandfather wanted to do was preach the Word one more time.

The same was true about my father. All throughout his ministry he was diligent to preach the Word. As I mentioned earlier, he gave me a Bible in which he wrote on the flyleaf, "Preach the Word." Eventually I went to Talbot Seminary because I wanted to study under Dr. Charles Feinberg. Dr. Feinberg was the most brilliant Bible scholar I knew. For example, he taught himself Dutch in two weeks so he could read a Dutch theology. He studied 14 years to be a rabbi and ended up being converted to Christ. He then attended Dallas Theological Seminary, where he earned his PhD. Dr. Lewis Sperry Chafer, who was the president of Dallas Theological

Seminary at that time, said of Dr. Feinberg that he was the only student who came to the seminary knowing more when he arrived than when he left.

Subsequently, Dr. Feinberg attended Johns Hopkins University to earn a PhD in archaeology. He had an immense and brilliant mind and he loved the Word of God. He read through the Bible four times a year and he was absolutely committed to the fact that every word of Scripture is inerrant, inspired, and true. He was the man I wanted to influence my life.

During my first year in seminary, my first class under Dr. Feinberg was Old Testament introduction. It was a demanding course that included a lot of tedious material which was hard to absorb for a college athlete who was suddenly exposed to academia. The first day a student asked a question, Dr. Feinberg dropped his head, never looked up, and said, "If you do not have a more intelligent question than that, do not ask any more questions. You are taking up valuable time." There were no more questions that semester! He had all the time to himself. He was dead serious about the things of God and Scripture.

That same year, I was assigned by Dr. Feinberg to preach a text before the student body and the faculty. I worked countless hours on this sermon. The faculty would sit behind you and write notes while you were preaching and then afterward they gave you their criticisms. I preached the message and thought I had done fine. When I was done, Dr. Feinberg handed me a sheet of paper with red writing across the front: "You missed the whole point of the passage."

How could I do that? How could I miss the whole point? That was the greatest lesson I ever had in seminary. Dr. Feinberg was upset and called me into his office because he wanted to make an investment in me and he did not appreciate what I had done. After all, handling God's Word correctly is the whole point of ministry. That day, I received a lecture I have never forgotten. Ever since, Dr. Feinberg has sat on my shoulder and whispered, "Do not miss the point of the passage, MacArthur!"

On graduation day, Dr. Feinberg called me into his office and said, "I have a gift for you." He picked up a big box, and in it were all 35 volumes of Keil and Delitzsch, a Hebrew Old Testament commentary set. He said, "This is the set I have used for years and years. I have all my notes in the margins; I want to give it to you as a gift." This was an expression of his love for me, but it was also another way of saying, "Now you have no excuse for missing the point of an Old Testament passage."

One of the highlights of my life was when Dr. Feinberg's family asked me to speak at his funeral. Somewhere along the line he must have told them that he thought I had finally gotten to the place where I could figure out the point of a passage. He is with the Lord now, but I do not want to do anything differently. I just want to continue doing what faithful prophets, apostles, preachers, evangelists, pastors, and missionaries have done through the ages. I am astonished at the boldness of people in ministry today who are quick to discard the God-ordained, scripturally mandated pattern of preaching and invent their own. What audacity! Who do they think they are?

So, preach the Word because of the devotion of the saints who came before you. Get in line, take the baton, and run your lap.

Preach the Word Because of the Dynamic of Scripture (3:15-17)

The third reason we preach the Word is because of the dynamic of Scripture. Paul wrote to Timothy, "From childhood you have known the sacred writings" (2 Timothy 3:15). From the time Timothy was a baby in his mother's arms, he was introduced to "the sacred writings." That is a Greek-Jewish term referring to the Old Testament, *hiera grammata*. Paul said, "You have known the [Old Testament, which is] able to give you the wisdom that leads to salvation through faith which is in Christ Jesus."

Although Timothy's parents were Jewish and Gentile, he still had the influence of the Old Testament law in his family. Paul was saying that since Timothy was a child, the law had been preparing him for the gospel. The Jews used to claim that their children "drank in" the law of God with their mother's milk and it was so imprinted on their hearts and minds that they would sooner forget their names than forget God's law.

The law was the tutor that led to Christ, and Timothy had been raised on the sacred writings of the Old Testament. He had been given the wisdom he needed so that when the gospel was preached, he apprehended it because his understanding of the Old Testament law prepared him for it. Ultimately, Paul was saying, "You know that the Word of God has the power to lead you to salvation. What else would you preach?" For it is sharper than any two-edged sword (Hebrews 4:12). Peter declared, "You have been born again…through the living and enduring Word of God" (1 Peter 1:23). It is the power of the Word that converts the soul and produces salvation.

You commit to preaching the Word when you understand that it is the power that converts the soul. If you do not preach the Word, then it's because you do not believe it is the only source of salvation and sanctification, no matter what you might claim otherwise. In 2 Timothy 3:16-17 we read, "All Scripture is inspired by God and profitable for teaching, for reproof, for correction, for training in righteousness; so that the man of God [and everyone who follows His pattern] may be adequate [or complete], equipped for every good work." It is the power of the Word that saves and sanctifies. It provides doctrine, it reproves error and sin, it sets upright, and it trains in the path of righteousness. That's the sequence.

Through preaching the Word you lay a foundation of doctrine and it reproves error and sin. In the original Greek text, this speaks of setting upright someone who has fallen down. You pick him back up, correct his error and his iniquity, and then put him on the path of righteousness. You train him to live an obedient life. It's the Word that makes the man of God and everybody who follows His pattern complete. It prepares them spiritually. This is what we call the sufficiency of Scripture—God's Word completely saves and completely sanctifies. What else would you use? I cannot fathom why anyone would use anything other than the Word that saves and sanctifies.

Preach the Word Because of the Demand of the Sovereign *(4:1-2)*

Next, we preach the Word because of the demand of the Sovereign. 2 Timothy 4:1 is a frightening verse that strikes me with holy fear. It should terrify every preacher. This verse helps us to understand why John Knox, before he ascended the pulpit to preach, fell on his face and burst forth in tears of fear. He was reverently afraid of misrepresenting the truth and knew he was under divine scrutiny. Paul wrote, "I solemnly charge you in the presence of God and of Christ Jesus, who is to judge the living and the dead, and by His appearing and His kingdom: preach the Word." The command "I solemnly charge you" is dead serious. Paul was commanding Timothy—and all preachers—with all solemnity and all seriousness.

"My friend," Paul said, "you are under the scrutiny of God, the one who will judge all who are alive and all who have died." The Greek construction here can be rendered "in the presence of God, even Jesus Christ," since He is introduced as the judge in the verse. We are preaching under the scrutiny of the omniscient and holy judge. I agree with what Paul wrote in 1 Corinthians 4:3-4: "It is a very small thing that I may be examined by you, or by any human court...the one who examines me is the Lord." A preacher cannot build his sense of faithfulness on whether his listeners like his sermon. He can appreciate his listeners' commendations and hear their criticisms, but in the end, he should preach to honor the One who is the judge. It is Christ who will reveal the secret things of the heart. He will give a reward to those who are worthy of it, and only His judgment matters.

A reporter once asked me, "For whom do you prepare your sermons?" I said, "To be truthful with you, I prepare them for God. He is the judge whom I have to stand before. He is the one who really matters. I want to get the message right before Him. I do not want to take the Word of the living God and somehow corrupt it, or replace it with foolish musings of my own."

Hebrews 13:17 says, "Obey your leaders and submit to them, for they keep watch over your souls as those who will give an account." Every minister will have to give an account someday before the Lord. I want to give my best to the Lord and build on the foundation with gold, silver, and precious stones (1 Corinthians 3:12). I want to receive that reward that evidences my love for Him, a reward I can cast at His feet in honor and praise. Someday we will all stand before that judgment seat for that time of reward for our labors.

It is a very serious thing for me, this matter of preaching. Sometimes people say to me, "You spend so much time in preparation. Why?" Because God's Word deserves it! We could probably get by with doing less because our listeners don't have high expectations. Frankly, with most listeners a few good stories will do it. But with God, the task of preaching is a different matter. When we preach, we must have Him in mind and the honor of His truth.

Preach the Word Because of the Deceptiveness of the Sensual *(4:3-4)*

Yet another reason we are to preach the Word is because of the deceptiveness of the sensual. The great enemy of the Word of God is anything outside the Word of God—the word of Satan, the word of demons, and the word of man. We are living in dangerous seasons concocted by seducing spirits and hypocritical liars. In 2 Timothy 4:3, Paul identifies for us that which makes it possible for false teachers to be successful: "The time will come when they will not endure sound doctrine." People will not want to hear healthy, wholesome teaching. They will not want the sound, solid teachings of the Word. They will just want their ears tickled. They will be driven by the sensual and not the cognitive. They won't be interested in truth or theology. Instead, they will want ear-tickling sensations rather than the great truths that save and sanctify. According to 2 Timothy 2:16, people will want to hear worldly and empty chatter that produces ungodliness and spreads like gangrene.

We are in such a season now. People say that teaching doctrine and being clear about the Word of God is divisive, unloving, and prideful. The prevailing mood in postmodern Western culture is that everyone determines truth for himself and everyone's opinion is as valid as everyone else's. There is no room for absolute, authoritative doctrine. That is one other "ism" you can add to the list of dangerous seasons—relativism.

**There will be no church left to fight anything
if we do not preserve the truth.**

Even the evangelical Christian church has fallen victim to this agenda. Many Christians are willing to speak up against abortion, homosexuality, and euthanasia. They are willing to fight for religious freedoms in America and, among other things, to preserve prayer in the schools. But the worst form of wickedness is the perversion of God's truth—that is, wrong doctrine and false teaching. The church today treats spiritual error with indifference as if it was harmless, as if a right interpretation of Scripture was unnecessary. While many Christians are fighting peripheral issues, they are giving away the essential truths that define our faith. That is suicide. There will be no church left to fight anything if we do not preserve the truth.

The ability to distinguish between truth and error is absolutely critical. You cannot speak truth or guard it if you do not understand it. That's why at our church we started The Master's Seminary—to train up men who can do that. These men do not worry about figuring out what is culturally relevant. They go all over the world with the Word of God, sort through the issues, and bring God's truth to bear upon the society in which they live. No matter what language you speak or where you live, everyone around you is in the same needy condition, spiritually destitute before God. And the truth of God transcends all cultures.

We live in a time when false teachers do not want to tell people the truth. They do not want to call error "error"; they do not want to confront sin because "they love you." But false teachers do not love their listeners. If they did, they would seek everyone's best and highest good and proclaim the truth of God's Word.

If I say, "I do not think it is loving to confront," then I do not love people. Rather, I am loving myself—I am more concerned about people liking me than about speaking the truth. It's more loving to confront people's error and show them the truth that can lead them to the blessings and well-being that produces God's greatest good in their lives. Instead we have a loss of truth, loss of conviction, loss of discernment, loss of holiness, loss of divine power, and loss of blessing—all because people want to get their ears tickled. "Tell me a little about success. Tell me a little about prosperity. Give me some excitement. Elevate my feelings of well-being, self-esteem, and give me emotional thrills." Second Timothy 4:3 says these people "will accumulate for themselves teachers in accordance to their own desires." The market creates the demand.

As Marvin Vincent said in *Word Studies in the New Testament,* "In periods of unsettled faith, skepticism and curious speculation in matters of religion, teachers of all kinds swarm like flies in Egypt. The demand creates the supply. The hearers invite and shape their own preachers. If the people desire a calf to worship, a ministerial calf maker can always be found."[3]

I was in Florida back when people were being rocked by the craziness that was going on in the name of revival and people were flipping and flopping around and diving on the floor and gyrating and speaking in bizarre and unintelligible ways. They kept saying, "This is all a work of God." Can I be straightforward with you? Such behavior is an offense to our rational, truth-revealing God. It is an offense to the true work of His Son. It is an offense to the true work of the Holy Spirit to use the names of God or of Christ or of the Holy Spirit in any mindless, emotional orgy marked by irrational, sensual, and fleshly behavior produced by altered states of consciousness, peer pressure, heightened expectation, or suggestibility. That is socio-psycho manipulation and mesmerism, and it is a prostitution of the glorious revelation of God taught clearly and powerfully to an eager, attentive, and controlled mind.

That which feeds sensual desires pragmatically or ecstatically cannot honor God. You have to preach the truth to the mind. That is where the real battle is fought. So we who are preachers are to bring God to people through His Word. That is the only way we can do it. People are starving for the knowledge of God—they just do not know it. But when we start delivering the truth, they find out. It was said of Bible expositor Martyn Lloyd-Jones, by J.I. Packer, "He brought more of the sense of God than any other man."[4] What a commendation!

PRAYER

Father, we thank You that we do not need to wander in some fog about the direction of life in ministry. We thank You that You have clarified it to us. We thank You that You are raising up men who will proclaim the truth. We thank You, Father, for their devotion and commitment to the fulfillment of this command.

O Lord, grant them power and faithfulness and integrity of life and effectiveness as they endeavor to serve You and carry out this commission. We thank You for men who will face the dangerous seasons, who maintain the devotion to the saints who went before them and were faithful, who will express the dynamic of the Word, who will discharge their responsibility before You as their Sovereign, and who will confront the desires of the sensual world with the powerful and rational truth of Scripture. Father, continue to raise them up, and we give You all the glory in Christ's name. Amen.

The Call of God

"He said to me, 'Son of man, take
into your heart all My words
which I speak to you and listen closely.'"

Ezekiel 3:10

2

THE CALL OF GOD

Mark Dever
Shepherds' Conference 2002
Ezekiel 1:28–3:15

I pastor a church in Washington, DC, of about 350 members, and we have approximately 400 to 500 attendees each Sunday morning. Because the church is located in the inner city, we have members from about 30 different countries. Our visitors range from congressmen to ambassadors. For a while we had one high-ranking official from the Chinese embassy who, for two years, celebrated Thanksgiving with my family. He had never attended a Christian church before visiting Capitol Hill. Ministering in this context has provided great opportunities for spreading the gospel.

I've also learned that diplomats are some of the most fascinating people in Washington. Historian Will Durant said, "To say nothing, especially when speaking, is half the art of diplomacy."[1] Now diplomats may think Durant's observation is harsh, but over the years I've read a few statements that support the point Durant was making. For example, President McKinley once asked an assistant secretary of state how to say no to six European ambassadors who were coming to see him about a certain matter. The career diplomat instantly grabbed an envelope and wrote this on the back of it:

The government of the United States appreciates the humanitarian and disinterested character of the communication now made on behalf of the powers named, and for its part is confident that equal appreciation will be shown for its own earnest and unselfish endeavors to fulfill a duty to humanity by ending a situation, the indefinite prolongation of which has become insufferable.[2]

The president read the message to each one of the ambassadors, and they were satisfied.

Another American president, Franklin Roosevelt, felt quite certain that politicians and diplomats rarely listen to each other. To prove his point, during a diplomatic reception, Roosevelt resolved to greet his guests who were standing in line by saying, "I murdered my grandmother this morning."[3] The story goes on to say that with only one exception, the president received very polite responses.

We're making sport of this a bit, but diplomacy is a serious matter—not just for Washington, but for everyone. We who are Americans tend to lean toward what's called "Wilsonianism," named after Woodrow Wilson, which advocates the idea that there's an underlying good in people and all we need to do is help reassert it. Henry Kissinger wrote a serious and important book on this topic entitled *Diplomacy*,[4] in which he argued against this ideology. Kissinger spent his career contending for Americans to have a more realistic outlook on humanity, assuming that even in the best of worlds there will still be clashes of interests.

Because conflict exists, we need diplomats—professional representatives who work sometimes for short-term advantage and sometimes for long-term interest. And as we turn our attention to the book of Ezekiel, we see the backdrop is a political conflict between the Babylonian Empire and Judah. Babylon had absorbed the little nation of Judah and begun to exile some of its citizens. However, the book of Ezekiel is not just about the conflict between Israel and Babylon, but more fundamentally about the conflict between Israel and God. As God's rebellious people continued in their insurgence, how would God react?

Some assume that God engages in a kind of religious diplomacy—that

He calls on religious professionals who read the latest polling information and use focus groups to determine how to market religion. These professionals usually conduct diplomacy on behalf of God by exacting a concession here and making a compromise there, equivocally bargaining for God and hoping something good may come out of it. This type of mindset deems that an individual strives to appear more reasonable and more diplomatic for God. If that's your idea of how God interacts with His people, then our study of Ezekiel should be of interest to you, particularly as a pastor.

Let's begin by reading Ezekiel 1:28–3:15:

> Such was the appearance of the likeness of the glory of the LORD. And when I saw it, I fell on my face and heard a voice speaking.
>
> Then He said to me, "Son of man, stand on your feet that I may speak with you!" As He spoke to me the Spirit entered me and set me on my feet; and I heard Him speaking to me. Then He said to me, "Son of man, I am sending you to the sons of Israel, to a rebellious people who have rebelled against Me; they and their fathers have transgressed against Me to this very day. I am sending you to them who are stubborn and obstinate children, and you shall say to them, 'Thus says the Lord GOD.' As for them, whether they listen or not—for they are a rebellious house—they will know that a prophet has been among them. And you, son of man, neither fear them nor fear their words, though thistles and thorns are with you and you sit on scorpions; neither fear their words nor be dismayed at their presence, for they are a rebellious house.
>
> "But you shall speak My words to them whether they listen or not, for they are rebellious. Now you, son of man, listen to what I am speaking to you; do not be rebellious like that rebellious house. Open your mouth and eat what I am giving you." Then I looked, and behold, a hand was extended to me; and lo, a scroll was in it. When He spread it out before me, it was

written on the front and back, and written on it were lamentations, mourning and woe.

Then He said to me, "Son of man, eat what you find; eat this scroll, and go, speak to the house of Israel." So I opened my mouth, and He fed me this scroll. He said to me, "Son of man, feed your stomach and fill your body with this scroll which I am giving you." Then I ate it, and it was sweet as honey in my mouth.

Then He said to me, "Son of man, go to the house of Israel and speak with My words to them. For you are not being sent to a people of unintelligible speech or difficult language, but to the house of Israel, nor to many peoples of unintelligible speech or difficult language, whose words you cannot understand. But I have sent you to them who should listen to you; yet the house of Israel will not be willing to listen to you, since they are not willing to listen to Me. Surely the whole house of Israel is stubborn and obstinate. Behold, I have made your face as hard as their faces and your forehead as hard as their foreheads. Like emery harder than flint I have made your forehead. Do not be afraid of them or be dismayed before them, though they are a rebellious house." Moreover, He said to me, "Son of man, take into your heart all My words which I will speak to you and listen closely. Go to the exiles, to the sons of your people, and speak to them and tell them, whether they listen or not, 'Thus says the Lord GOD.'"

Then the Spirit lifted me up, and I heard a great rumbling sound behind me, "Blessed be the glory of the LORD in His place." And I heard the sound of the wings of the living beings touching one another and the sound of the wheels beside them, even a great rumbling sound. So the Spirit lifted me up and took me away; and I went embittered in the rage of my spirit, and the hand of the LORD was strong on me. Then I came to the exiles who lived beside the river Chebar at Tel-abib, and I sat there seven days where they were living, causing consternation among them.

At the outset of our study, we need to recognize that our call to be a pastor was not exactly like Ezekiel's call. Too often when we go to the Old Testament we attempt to draw direct correlations between biblical characters and ourselves—correlations that aren't necessarily accurate. A look at the Old Testament for exemplary purposes is fine, for Paul sanctioned this in his letter to the Corinthians when he said, "These things happened as examples for us" (1 Corinthians 10:6). Yet at the same time, we will not find exact parallels between Ezekiel's commission and ours. Even so, there are some details in this text that are instructive for us. If we are called to be messengers, ministers, and teachers of God's Word, then we must consider four statements from this passage that will benefit us, our ministries, and those to whom we minister.

The Message Must Be the Word of God

A very important aspect of our calling as pastors is that the message we proclaim must be the Word of God. One who serves as a messenger is not called to be inventive. Rather, he is commissioned to give God's words alone. One reason I like the Puritans so much is that they valued plainness. If you were to tell a Puritan pastor that you thought he was painful, pathetic, and plain, you'd be giving him a high compliment. *Painful* entails taking pains in ministry. *Pathetic* entails feeling for the flock. *Being plain* means not drawing attention to yourself, but dealing straight with another's soul.

It is this kind of plainness that God was calling Ezekiel to demonstrate. Ezekiel was to be, if you will, the donkey on which Christ sat to ride into Jerusalem. The prophet was simply to bear the Word of God, and the scroll mentioned in Ezekiel 2:9 symbolized this. The scroll is a picture of God's Word, which came to Ezekiel before it went out to the people. The question, however, was this: Would Ezekiel receive the Word of God?

Unlike the rebellious house of Israel, Ezekiel was obedient to God's instructions. He passed the test. Let's look at the details of his reaction in Ezekiel 1:28–2:2:

> When I saw it, I fell on my face and heard a voice speaking. Then He said to me, "Son of man, stand on your feet that I may

speak with you!" As He spoke to me the Spirit entered me and set me on my feet.

God set Ezekiel on his feet because He wanted the prophet to be clearheaded and able to concentrate in order to understand the message he was about to receive. Unlike what happens in pagan religious experiences, Ezekiel would be required to have a clear mind. He was not to be in a trance or a frenzy, but instead, in a heightened state of alertness. As a result, the prophet would need to get up on his feet and listen.

The Word given to Ezekiel included lament and woe:

> "Now you, son of man, listen to what I am speaking to you; do not be rebellious like that rebellious house. Open your mouth and eat what I am giving you." Then I looked, and behold, a hand was extended to me; and lo, a scroll was in it. When He spread it out before me, it was written on the front and back, and written on it were lamentations, mourning and woe (Ezekiel 2:8-10).

Sometimes the message God has for His people is a difficult one, but friend, if it is God's Word, we do His people no service by altering it or refusing to give it.

The pastor and evangelist A.B. Earle said that the text he found most blessed of God for the conversion of souls in his ministry was Mark 3:29: "Whoever blasphemes against the Holy Spirit never has forgiveness, but is guilty of an eternal sin."[5] Jonathan Edwards said he found Romans 3:19 to be most used by God for the conversion of souls in his ministry: "Now we know that whatever the Law says, it speaks to those who are under the Law, so that every mouth may be closed and all the world may become accountable to God."[6] God's people need to know the whole truth. He will use the message that we preach, even when the content is burdensome. We must know and teach the things our people don't want to hear. We need to make sure that our message is the Word of God, and nothing more. We have to be willing to say, "God, whatever You're speaking, I will give out. If it's in Your Word, I will preach it, and I will not go beyond it by presenting something that is *not* the Word of God as *the* Word of God."

God was not commissioning Ezekiel to go around and give religious lectures on whatever topics he desired. Ezekiel was a messenger of God only as long as he gave God's message. If he had begun to declare anything else, then he would have ceased to be God's herald. You see this in the following passages:

> Ezekiel 2:4—"I am sending you to them who are stubborn and obstinate children, and you shall say to them, '*Thus says the Lord* GOD.'"

> Ezekiel 3:4—"Go to the house of Israel and speak with *My words* to them."

> Ezekiel 3:11—"Go to the exiles, to the sons of your people, and speak to them and tell them, whether they listen or not, '*Thus says the Lord* GOD'" (emphasis mine).

God told Ezekiel to listen, to eat, to take heart, and then to go and speak. It was not that Ezekiel was extremely insightful and so God decided that he should go on the lecture circuit. No, Ezekiel was a priest trained in God's law and had been taken into captivity and exile in Babylon, but God called him to be a prophet. He received this calling not because of his own insight, but because of God's will.

Anyone who claims to be called to ministry has to realize that he is God's messenger only as long as he gives His message.

If you are a minister of God's Word, beware of the danger in misusing your position. Anyone who claims to be called to ministry has to realize that he is God's messenger only as long as he gives His message. We're not called to be preachers in a sense that we can preach whatever we want, any more than we would appreciate it if our mailman started scribbling notes to us and then sending them through our door or mailbox. The mailman is valuable to us only as long as he faithfully delivers to us the mail that others have sent.

I hope you haven't been scribbling down your own thoughts and presenting them to God's people as if they were God's words. If there's one person in the universe whose mouth I would not want to put my words into, it would be God. When you are standing in front of God's people, make sure it is God's Word you are giving to them. Be careful of the things that you identify as an essential part of Christianity which are not, and be careful of the things that you claim His Word is saying.

The Messenger Must Be Sympathetic

A French diplomat was on the verge of taking up a new ambassadorship when he visited President Charles de Gaulle and said to him, "I'm filled with joy at my appointment," to which De Gaulle responded with a frown, "You are a career diplomat, joy is an inappropriate emotion in your profession."[7] In our passage, we see that Ezekiel was no diplomat. He was not called to be a casual professional in his negotiations between God and His rebellious people; instead, as the messenger, he was to be sympathetic. That's the second statement we must consider as ministers.

In this passage, Ezekiel is sympathetic to the recipients of the message. It's interesting that though Ezekiel says that God's Words tasted "sweet as honey in my mouth" (3:3), his reaction afterward was that he "went embittered in the rage of my spirit" (verse 14). Why is that?

I think Ezekiel went away in bitterness because he was sad for his people. The message Ezekiel was called to bear, at least initially, was a tough one, and he doesn't have any *Schadenfreude*—that is, enjoyment over someone else's pain. Instead, Ezekiel has sympathy. It's only natural that he didn't want to be a bearer of bad news. Likewise, sin or the denunciation of it is never something to delight in. Consider your own ministry—when you see a brother or sister caught in sin, do you savor the thought of needing to confront him or her? Of course you delight in the fact that God loves His people and that they can be freed from their sin. But do you relish the actual work of being that messenger?

In a similar fashion, Ezekiel didn't relish being the messenger to a stubborn and obstinate people. God told Ezekiel that He had an important message for the people of Israel, yet the people wouldn't listen to it. Ezekiel could not have appreciated this aspect of his task. Yet the reality is that God doesn't only want His Word to go to white fields of harvest. His purpose is for His Word to go everywhere—even to some of the most difficult, dangerous, and unresponsive people in the world.

We should expect to experience dread when we find it necessary to counsel parents with intractable children or minister to people who are caught in sin. It's difficult when we know the people we are about to address are likely to be resistant or unresponsive. So we can relate to why Ezekiel would have a bitter spirit toward the task he was being called to, or why he felt overwhelmed by it.

I remember attending a conference a number of years ago at which the speaker gave a very clear talk on hell. I recall walking out afterward and hearing people say in a lighthearted manner, "Wasn't it great to hear such a clear word on hell?" I knew what they meant because we hear so little with regard to the topic of hell today, and the message was beneficial. But there was nothing qualifying that in their voices. I thought, *Surely these people couldn't have contemplated the reality of exactly what they had just heard.* To clarify, I didn't disagree with the speaker at all, and I too was thankful to have heard his message. But I couldn't imagine being happy about it in the way other people were. The thought of hell and what it means for unrepentant sinners must provoke sympathy.

Please understand that I agree with Jonathan Edwards when he says that God will be glorified in the damnation of sinners.[8] But I am not in heaven yet. My heart is not yet perfectly holy and my sympathies are not yet entirely where they should be. Our Lord Jesus, while hanging on the cross and displaying God's glorious justice and mercy, did not laugh as He was bearing our sorrows. Rather, He was sympathetic, and we who are God's messengers should likewise have sympathy toward those to whom we're proclaiming God's Word. Even though our message may be an unfavorable one, we must not be harsh with the recipients.

Ezekiel's sympathy toward his audience was motivated by another factor—God's sympathy. As an individual meditates on Scripture, his mind and heart become conformed to God's mind and heart. Similarly, as Ezekiel took in the message of God's judgment, he began to be conformed to

God's feelings toward His people. Ezekiel internalized this word of judgment and was compelled to feel as God felt about the people's disobedience. At the same time, he did not let his feelings bend God's hard truths. He was true to God's message, and we should be as well. We must be faithful for the sake of our people, and we must also be faithful for God's sake.

As a pastor, will you direct all your sympathies toward people and none to God? Are you tempted to condemn God as being too harsh when you read certain passages of Scripture? Let me suggest that instead of trying to exculpate God and make Him not guilty of something that you perceive Him to be guilty of, why not pause and try to have sympathy toward God? Assume for a moment that He is right, that He is infinitely holy, and that He can justly require everything of us, and then see what that does to your assessment of the situation. As God's messengers, we should have sympathy with God. I'm not saying God needs to be the object of our pity. Rather, we must share our Father's perspective. We must have a concern for His name, glory, and honor.

When it is necessary to confront someone, don't become preoccupied with how that person might be offended by your message. Instead, think about how God is hurt, how He is offended. After all, sin is a personal revolt against God and His lordship. If we are to be His messengers, we must be sympathetic not only to people but also to God, our Creator and Redeemer.

The Messenger Must Know that God Will Supply

If the heart and soul of our ministry is preaching the Bible, then we don't have to worry about running out of things to say. God's Word is inexhaustible, and He is fully sufficient to supply everything needed. As we've seen, God supplied His Word to Ezekiel, and we read in Ezekiel 3:14 that He also supplied a way: "The Spirit lifted me up and took me away." God took the prophet to a specific location and promised to empower him to fulfill his mission. He equipped Ezekiel with the courage to address a hard and stubborn people:

> As for them, whether they listen or not—for they are a rebellious house—they will know that a prophet has been among

them. And you, son of man, neither fear them nor fear their words, though thistles and thorns are with you and you sit on scorpions; neither fear their words nor be dismayed at their presence, for they are a rebellious house (2:5-6).

God went on to tell Ezekiel, "The house of Israel will not be willing to listen to you, since they are not willing to listen to Me. Surely the whole house of Israel is stubborn and obstinate. Behold, I have made your face as hard as their faces and your forehead as hard as their foreheads. Like emery harder than flint I have made your forehead" (3:7-9).

Because Israel was rebellious, God promised to harden Ezekiel so he would be prepared to carry out his task. What God begins He will complete—He will provide the strength His messenger needs to stay the course. When God told Ezekiel to speak, He gave Ezekiel the words. When God told Ezekiel to go, He took him to the location. When God told Ezekiel that the people would be hard, He promised to make Ezekiel harder still. As a result, Ezekiel's determination to speak was tougher than the people's refusal to listen.

Pastors cannot rely on their own ability, but on God's. Augustine prayed, "Give me the grace to do as You command, and command me to do as You will."[9] That should be our prayer as well.

I'm reminded of an interaction I had with someone early in my pastoral ministry. During a church potluck, I sat down next to one of the older members of the church—someone who didn't seem to like me. This member turned to me and said, "I don't like young pastors." I calmly responded, "Really?" and continued to eat. Then he said, "Well, I might make an exception in your case." I turned and said, "I guess you've seen a good number of pastors come and go, haven't you?"

"Yes," he replied.

At which time I said, "Well, I think you may have met your match." Then I turned back to eating my meal.

Sometimes a holy resolve, not a discourteous hardness, is exactly what the Lord calls us to. If He has made you a messenger to a hard and obstinate people, He must in some ways make you harder and more obstinate. I'm not encouraging you to indulge in sinful selfishness, arrogance, impatience, or immaturity as you carry out your task. But understand that when the way is hard, God will supply the stamina you need. You have never been and you will never be in a situation beyond what God can enable you to bear. Pray that He will enable you to endure, and know that He will supply.

The Messenger Must Expect Rejection

The final statement we must consider is that the messenger of God must expect rejection. One of the more interesting details about the book of Ezekiel is the frequent use of the title "son of man." It's used 93 times, and scholars have spilt endless amounts of ink speculating on what all might be involved in its meaning. The title "son of man" seems to mean mortal or subject to death, and it often tends to be associated with rejection. Ezekiel refers to himself as "son of man" because he understood himself to be the rejected ambassador of a rejected King.

Ezekiel was not the only one in the Old Testament who faced rejection. Isaiah presented the Suffering Servant as a rejected individual: "He has no stately form or majesty that we should look upon Him, nor appearance that we should be attracted to Him. He was despised and forsaken of men, a man of sorrows and acquainted with grief; and like one from whom men hide their face He was despised, and we did not esteem Him" (53:2-3). In this way Isaiah prophesied that the Messiah would be despised and rejected. So it's no surprise that it was common for Jesus to refer to Himself by the title "Son of Man." For example, we read in Mark 8:31, "He began to teach them that the Son of Man must suffer many things and be rejected by the elders and the chief priests and the scribes, and be killed, and after three days rise again."

A little later in Mark 9:31 we read, "He was teaching His disciples and telling them, 'The Son of Man is to be delivered into the hands of men, and they will kill Him; and when He has been killed, He will rise three days later.'" Jesus then used this title again in Mark 10:33-34:

> Behold, we are going up to Jerusalem, and the Son of Man will be delivered to the chief priests and the scribes; and they will condemn Him to death and will hand Him over to the

Gentiles. They will mock Him and spit on Him, and scourge Him and kill Him, and three days later He will rise again.

By adopting the title "Son of Man," Jesus was affirming a long tradition of rejection, a rejection that He explained by quoting Psalm 22:1, "My God, my God, why have You forsaken me?" and Psalm 118:22, "The stone which the builders rejected has become the cornerstone." If you want to survive in the ministry, you must witness the rejection that Jesus experienced. You must reflect on His ministry. You must not allow the carnality in your own heart to entice you to find a way to be more successful in ministry than Jesus was.

Suffering is common to believers. The entire letter of 1 Peter was written to disperse any confusion Christians had with regard to their trials. Confusion exists because suffering seems to be counterintuitive. The logic some have is that when we turn to God, we should experience blessings and not trials. But Scripture tells us the people in the first-century church experienced suffering. Peter encouraged some of these people by saying to them in 1 Peter 2:20-21, "When you do what is right and suffer for it [and] you patiently endure it, this finds favor with God. For you have been called for this purpose, since Christ also suffered for you, leaving you an example for you to follow in His steps."

In other words, "Don't be discouraged because of your suffering. If you're suffering for doing good, that's a sign you're on the right path. Look at who you're following. What happened to Him? Did He receive universal acceptance and acclaim? No, He knew rejection and suffering."

Appealing to Christ's example, Peter then charged his fellow believers with the following words:

> Beloved, do not be surprised at the fiery ordeal among you, which comes upon you for your testing, as though some strange thing were happening to you; but to the degree that you share the sufferings of Christ, keep on rejoicing, so that also at the revelation of His glory you may rejoice with exultation (1 Peter 4:12-13).

Now it's true that some of the suffering we face is due to our own stupidity. Even a great minister like Jonathan Edwards made foolish mistakes as a pastor. When he was fired from his church in North Hampton, it wasn't only because he was faithful to preach God's Word. He had also publicly summoned some of the children of the prominent families to talk to him in connection with a scandalous matter, unintentionally implying that the kids were guilty of some heinous crime. Edwards made relatively small pastoral mistakes that resulted in major consequences.

**If you are presenting the gospel in a way
that makes it attractive to a carnal person,
then you're setting your church up to misunderstand
what it means to follow Christ.**

Although some of the suffering we experience is brought upon ourselves, there's still more that's encountered in the midst of faithful ministry. It is normal for the messenger of God's Word to face rejection in a fallen world. If you are presenting the gospel in a way that makes it attractive to a carnal person, then you're setting your church up to misunderstand what it means to follow Christ. The faithful preaching of God's Word will result in some rejection.

Now, even though rejection is normal, it is not final. Praise God for such a hope! Read with me another reference to the title "Son of Man"—one that appears in Daniel 7:13-14:

> I kept looking in the night visions, and behold, with the clouds
> of heaven One like a Son of Man was coming, and He came
> up to the Ancient of Days and was presented before Him. And
> to Him was given dominion, glory and a kingdom, that all the
> peoples, nations and men of every language might serve Him.
> His dominion is an everlasting dominion which will not pass
> away; and His kingdom is one which will not be destroyed.

In the New Testament we see who this "Son of Man" is. When Jesus was asked whether He was the Messiah, He said to the high priest, "I am; and you shall see the Son of Man sitting at the right hand of power, and coming with the clouds of heaven" (Mark 14:62). The Suffering Servant is also the glorious King. The pattern you see in the teaching of Jesus, in the book of Acts, in 1 Peter, and in other places in the Bible is suffering, *then* glory. Beware when someone comes preaching just glory. But you also don't want someone who preaches just suffering. For suffering is followed by glory.

There is nothing we will suffer in the ministry that we will not be repaid for infinitely. From the shores of heaven we will look back and say, "Oh, it was worth it a thousand times over." That's why we look at Jesus' entrance into Jerusalem during the passion week and we call it the triumphal entry. We know He's going to be betrayed and killed, but we also know that it is not the whole story. Jesus would rise from the dead, ascend into heaven, and will reign there until He comes back and gathers the universe to worship Him.

So if you have been called to serve as one of His messengers, remember these words: "Let us...[fix] our eyes on Jesus, the author and perfecter of faith, who for the joy set before Him endured the cross, despising the shame, and has sat down at the right hand of the throne of God. For consider Him who has endured such hostility by sinners against Himself, so that you will not grow weary and lose heart" (Hebrews 12:2-3).

PRAYER

God, You know the weariness that Your messengers can feel—a weariness that goes far beyond the physical. We pray, Lord, that any opposition that we have experienced from sinful men will be put in perspective as we consider Him who endured such opposition. O God, give us hearts that are fixed on the presentation of the Lord Jesus Christ in Your Word. Give us the time, patience, and discipline to meditate on Christ. Help us to understand further how to follow Christ and to be Your messengers. Work in our hearts by Your Spirit in a way that You would never work through the eloquence of a speaker or through the accuracy of descriptions in a book, but only as Your Holy Spirit can work through our hearts, through each one of our situations, so that you may receive all the glory. In Jesus' name we pray, Amen.

EPITAPH OF A FAITHFUL PREACHER

"I have fought the good fight, I have finished
the course, I have kept the faith."

2 TIMOTHY 4:7

3

EPITAPH OF A FAITHFUL PREACHER

John MacArthur

Shepherds' Conference 2003

2 Timothy 4:6-8

The words of dying men tend to be stripped of all hypocrisy—they tend to reveal what resides within a man's heart. For example, Napoleon, on his deathbed, said, "I die before my time and my body will be given back to earth to become the food of worms, such is the fate which so soon awaits the great Napoleon."[1] It was Mahatma Gandhi who said, at the edge of his death, "My days are numbered. For the first time in fifty years I find myself in a slew of despond, all about me is darkness, I am praying for light." What's interesting is that the phrase "slew of despond" comes from *The Pilgrim's Progress*, which Gandhi had read but not believed. It was Charles Maurice de Talleyrand, a prominent French diplomat of the nineteenth century, who wrote on a piece of paper that was found after his death, "What cares, what agitation, what anxieties, what ill will, what sad complications, and all this without other results except great fatigue of mind, and body, and a profound sentiment of discouragement with regard to the future, and disgust with regard to the past."[2] Such miserable ways to die! Yet there are better ways to die.

I remember, in my childhood, visiting Christ Church in Philadelphia. As I wandered around the church grounds I found the gravestone of Benjamin Franklin. I cannot vouch for the purity of his religion, but I liked the epitaph he wrote for himself—so much so that I memorized it:

The Body of
B. Franklin, Printer.
Like the Cover of an old Book,
Its Contents torn out,
And Stript of its Lettering & Gilding,
Lies here, Food for Worms.
But the Work shall not be lost:
For it will, as he believ'd,
appear once more
In a new and more elegant Edition,
Corrected and Improved
By the Author.[3]

Like Ben Franklin, the apostle Paul wrote his own epitaph. Here's what he said:

I am already being poured out as a drink offering, and the time of my departure has come. I have fought the good fight, I have finished the course, I have kept the faith; in the future there is laid up for me the crown of righteousness, which the Lord, the righteous judge, will award to me on that day; and not only to me, but also to all who have loved His appearing (2 Timothy 4:6-8).

Faithful to the End

I want to take you not to the next few years of your ministry, but to the end of your life. I want you to think about what your epitaph will say. Second Timothy 4:6-8 contains the epitaph of God's greatest servant among men; here we find Paul's own assessment of his life. When he wrote it, he was on the brink of death—his trial had taken place, his sentence was death, and his execution was imminent. Paul knew his present imprisonment would be his last, and that he was on his way to martyrdom.

I suppose by human standards it wasn't a good time for Paul to leave the world. I am sure that among many believers in the early church, there was a deep and profound love and affection for this apostle. After all, many Gentile believers were able to trace their spiritual lineage back to his ministry—they were indebted to him because he had introduced them to Christ as their Savior. Who could ever replace him? He was the last of the apostles, and there was no apostolic succession after him. Paul had firsthand experiences with the risen Jesus on several occasions, the first being on the road to Damascus. There was nobody like him, and yet it was now time for him to go.

Paul's departure took place at a seemingly inappropriate time for the church. For example, the church at Ephesus, where Timothy was pastoring, had fallen upon difficult times. Paul had started this church, and it had gotten to the point where people were deviating from the truth and abandoning the pursuit of holy things, and corrupt leaders were leading people astray. As a result, the church was erring in doctrine and conduct. That's why Paul had left Timothy in charge—he hoped that Timothy would set things right. But the resistance from within the church and persecution from outside evidently had caused Timothy to waver.

In the beginning of the letter that bears his epitaph, Paul wrote to Timothy, "I am mindful of the sincere faith within you" (2 Timothy 1:5). That's an interesting statement—it's like writing a letter to someone and saying, "Dear friend, I know you're a Christian, but..." Why else would Paul remind Timothy that the young disciple was in the faith, unless there were certain things happening that might call that into question?

Paul then went on to explain why he mentioned Timothy's "sincere faith": "For this reason I remind you to kindle afresh the gift of God, which is in you" (1:6). He was saying, "Timothy, you have a gift for preaching and ministry, which was affirmed by the elders of the church. Stir it up." Paul was rightly concerned because Timothy had evidently faltered in the use of his gifts. Because of pressure from the inside and persecution from the outside, he was beginning to collapse. That's why, in the next verse, Paul gave this exhortation: "God has not given us a spirit of timidity" (1:7). When Paul spoke of Timothy's "timidity," he was referring to cowardice. This was very serious—not only because Paul, the last of the apostles, was on the verge of leaving, but because Paul's replacement, Timothy, was waning. It had gotten to the point Paul found it necessary to say, "Don't be a coward. Keep doing what you've been gifted to do." In verse 8 Paul added, "Don't be ashamed of the testimony of our Lord."

A few verses later Paul urged, "Retain the standard of sound words. Guard, through the Holy Spirit who dwells in us, the treasure which has been entrusted to you" (1:13-14). When you're under persecution from outsiders and resistance from within the church, you'll find yourself tempted to change your doctrine and compromise so that you can ease up some of the pressure on you. But Paul told Timothy to combat that temptation and guard what had been entrusted to him.

We get a sense for how dire the situation might have been when Paul added, "You are aware of the fact that all who are in Asia [have] turned away from me" (1:15). The implication is, "Timothy, are you also going to turn away?"

This is strong language from Paul. It reveals the condition of Timothy's heart and the health of the Ephesian church. Paul had given Timothy the responsibility of leading in Ephesus and being an example to the other churches. Yet Timothy was drifting toward weakness. That's why in 2 Timothy 2:1 Paul wrote, "You therefore, my son, be strong in the grace that is in Christ Jesus." In the verses that follow he urged, "Be a soldier," "Be an athlete," "Be a hardworking farmer," "Be a diligent workman," "Be a vessel for honor and flee youthful lusts," and "Be a slave of the Lord." Paul commanded Timothy to not give in, fail, or compromise.

In the next chapter, Paul wrote, "Continue in the things you have learned" (3:14). Contextually, it is important to remember that in 2 Timothy 3:16 Paul reminded Timothy that all Scripture was inspired by God and was profitable for every good work. Then in 4:2 Paul exhorted this young man to "preach the word." This entire epistle of 2 Timothy was an attempt by the apostle Paul, under the inspiration of the Holy Spirit, to infuse strength into a weakened Timothy.

You can see, then, that from a human perspective, this was not the optimal time for the apostle Paul to depart. Yet Paul went on to express a quiet confidence as he prepared to step aside and let Timothy succeed him. After boldly confronting Timothy, Paul then exhibited an attitude of triumphant victory as he summed up his life with these words: "I have fought the good fight, I have finished the course, I have kept the faith" (4:7). In essence, Paul was saying, "I am ready to go."

You can't control the next generation, and you can't determine what will happen after you're gone. As it turned out, Paul's concern about the church at Ephesus proved to be legitimate. By the time the book of Revelation was written, we learn that this church had left its first love. This prompted Jesus to say, "I am coming to you and will remove your lampstand out of its place—unless you repent" (Revelation 2:5).

Even when Paul had plenty of reason for concern, he faced death triumphantly. He was able to look back over his life and say, "I did what the Lord asked me to do, and that's all I can do. I can't guarantee the future; I can't guarantee the successor. I can only do what I was given to do."

Paul's Epitaph

In his epitaph, Paul viewed his life from three perspectives: the present, the past, and the future. He looked to the close of his life, the course of his life, and the future of his life. He did this not merely to provide information for Timothy, but to motivate him. There was nothing subtle about what Paul wrote to this young man who was likely wavering: "I am going to run and fight to the end. I am going to keep the faith." Such words would have served as a strong encouragement to Timothy.

**For a soldier to have motivation
to fight in the moment, he needs to have
victory in view at the end.**

The New Testament tells us that Paul was put in prison for his faithfulness. In this way he was an effective role model for Timothy, and that should be true for us as well. Paul is our example when it comes to finishing strong. I can't think about the next week or next month of my life without thinking about the end. It's what I want to be at the end that keeps me on course right now.

The metaphors Paul used in 2 Timothy 2 reaffirm this idea. For a soldier to have motivation to fight in the moment, he needs to have victory in view at the end. For an athlete to exert himself in the middle of a race, he needs to keep in mind the reward that comes with winning the race. Any steward given a responsibility finds it helpful to remember he will have to give an account for how he guarded what was entrusted to him. It's our view of the end that sustains us in the present.

When ministers default doctrinally or morally—when they wander away from their calling—it's usually because they've lost sight of the end. They've stopped looking ahead to the final victory, the final reward, the final affirmation.

If you have a clear view of the way you want to finish, then you will know how to move forward. If you care about winning, then you will know how you need to run. With that in mind, let's look at Paul's three perspectives for finishing well.

The Close of Paul's Life: Poured Out as an Offering

In his epitaph, Paul looked first at the present aspect of his life: "I am already being poured out as a drink offering, and the time of my departure has come" (2 Timothy 4:6). The confidence he expressed here is remarkable. He said, "It's over. I am being poured out, and the time has come." In the original Greek text the word translated "time" is *kiros*, which is not a reference to time as measured on a clock, but to an epoch or an era. Paul was saying, "The season of my departure has come."

Note that Paul said he was "being poured out as a drink offering." Here, he used Jewish language from the Old Testament. When the children of Israel went into the land of Canaan, God gave them instructions on how to conduct worship. This included guidelines for the burnt offering (Numbers 15). This was an offering for sin—it was recognition on the part of the people that the wages of sin was death, and that there was a need for a sacrifice to pay for their sins. This sacrifice pointed toward the Lord Jesus Christ, the one and only true sacrifice. But before Christ's death on the cross, the burnt offering involved putting a slain animal on the altar as an offering to God.

But the slain animal wasn't placed alone on the altar. Poured over the offering was flour mixed with oil, which produced a sweet aroma. And wine was added to all this as well. Paul had this imagery in mind when he said, "I gave myself as a burnt offering. I put my whole life up there—all of it from the Damascus Road onward. For the last three decades I've been up there on that altar, offering up my life and taking no thought for myself. For me, to live is Christ and to die is gain. If I live, I live to the Lord and if I die, I die to the Lord. Whatever happens, I am the Lord's."

This imagery is beautiful. The burnt offering symbolizes Paul's life, and the drink offering symbolizes his death. Paul understood sacrifice, and that's why he could live the way he did. That's why he could fight the good fight, run the race, and maintain his stewardship all the way to the end— he had never viewed his life as his own. For Paul, life wasn't about success or accolades or prestige. It was about sacrifice.

In Romans 12:1, Paul wrote, "Present your bodies a living and holy sacrifice, acceptable to God, which is your spiritual service of worship." He practiced what he preached and gave his body as a living sacrifice wholly acceptable to God. When you approach life that way, there's no disappointment when things don't go according to plan. Rather than pursue comfort, you're more concerned about giving your life away—and as a result, you're not worried about becoming burned out.

Earlier, in Philippians 2:17, when Paul wrote "Even if I am being poured out as a drink offering," he was speaking hypothetically. But here in 2 Timothy 4:6, the language is not hypothetical; it is real. Don't think for a moment there was anything easy about what Paul faced. He was in prison, winter was coming, and it would soon be very cold. That's why in 2 Timothy 4:13 he said, "Bring the cloak which I left at Troas." If Paul survived through the winter before his execution, it was going to be cold and he wouldn't have anything to read, so he asked for both his cloak and "the books, especially the parchments."

As if that weren't enough, Paul also faced serious opposition: "Alexander the coppersmith did me much harm" (4:14). Timothy was to watch out for Alexander because he vigorously opposed biblical teaching. Paul then added, "At my first defense no one supported me, but all deserted me...But the Lord stood with me" (2 Timothy 4:16-17). Paul had been abandoned and was lonely. This had to be difficult for him. Is this how the great apostle ended his ministry? Nobody was naming cathedrals after him then. He was alone, forsaken by Demas and others. Because he was lonely, Paul asked for Mark and for something to read. Even at the end of his life, Paul was an offering on the altar.

Paul then said, "The time of my departure has come" (2 Timothy 4:6). "Has come" is in the perfect verb tense in the original Greek text, which means it had already come, or it had already arrived. The clouds of death were already hovering over Paul. I love his use of the word "departure" (Greek, *analyseōs*)—that's a great way to view death. When we use the word *departure*, we don't usually think about it in the context of death. Rather, we use the word in the sense of leaving one location and going to another. That's exactly what Paul meant, but he had his death in mind. It's interesting to note that in the New Testament, *analyseōs* was used in a number of ways that fit with the point Paul was making.

First, *analyseōs* was used to speak of unyoking an animal from the shaft of a plow. Paul viewed death as being unhooked from all the toil he had exerted here on earth. He would soon be able to lay down his heavy load of ministry.

Second, *analyseōs* was used in reference to the loosening of chains, fetters, or bonds that held a prisoner. In essence, Paul was saying, "Not only am I going to be loosed from the burden of my labor, I'm also going to be loosed from the chains of my fallenness, my persecution, and all else that binds me. I will be released from the confines of my flesh and this Roman prison and enter into the glorious liberty of the courts of heaven."

Third, *analyseōs* was used to speak of bringing down a tent. The nomadic people in Bible lands would put up a tent, live in that location for a brief time, then take their tent down. Paul was saying, "I'm about to take this tent down, and I won't be putting it up again. I'm going to live in a place where there aren't any tents. I'm going to the dwelling place prepared for me in the Father's house, where I will live in the glories of heaven forever."

Fourth, *analyseōs* was used in connection with the loosening of a ship's mooring ropes. Many times during his missionary journeys crisscrossing the Mediterranean, Paul had stood on a deck and watched the ropes fall away as the ship began to move out to sea. This, however, would be the last time Paul set sail, launching him into the greatest deep of all—crossing the waters of death and arriving at the port of heaven.

For the Christian, death means laying down every burden and labor in exchange for a rest that lasts forever. It also means the laying aside of all the sins and difficulties that bind and pull. Death is striking camp, as it were, to take up residence in a permanent place, an eternal home. It is casting off the ropes that bind us to this world and sailing into God's world, where we will live in His presence forever. And here in 2 Timothy 4, Paul declares, "I'm ready for that!"

Wouldn't it be great to come to the end of your life and be able to say, "I'm done, Lord. What is the delay?" This reminds me of Robert Browning's poem about a young soldier who came flying from the battlefield to report to Napoleon the victory at Ratisbon. Though he was wounded, the soldier was eager to bring the good news to his chief. Napoleon noticed the man's wounds and the poem ends with these now-famous lines:

> "You're wounded!" "Nay," the soldier's pride
> Touch'd to the quick, he said:
> "I'm kill'd, Sire!" And his chief beside,
> Smiling the boy fell dead.[4]

The soldier's message was, "No sir, I'm not wounded, I'm proud to be dead for your cause." The apostle Paul was saying something similar: "I've done my duty; now I lay down my life."

The Course of Paul's Life: Committed to a Fight

In 2 Timothy 4:7 Paul looked to his past and said, "I have fought the good fight, I have finished the course, I have kept the faith." In the original Greek text, all those verbs are in the perfect tense, describing actions completed in the past and bearing present results. Actually, the order of the words in the Greek text is "The good fight I have fought, the course I have finished, the faith I have kept." In each case, the object is placed before the verb so that the emphasis is on the object. That was how Paul viewed ministry: as a course, a faith, a body of truth, a race to run, and a battle to fight.

Wouldn't it be great to look back over your life and have no regrets? No sadness, no lack of fulfillment, no feeling of having left things unfinished? Paul faced death with complete satisfaction and triumph. I can't think of a more glorious way to leave this world. I don't know how you think about death, but I assume most people think about it in terms of its physical reality. People exercise, eat healthy, and do whatever it takes to protect their heart and body and ensure they don't die young. They do whatever they can to protect themselves physically.

When it comes to death, I don't know how I'm going to go—that's all in God's hands. But when I consider death, I don't think so much about the physical aspect of it. Rather, I'm more concerned with the spiritual aspect. Where will I be in terms of my faithfulness when my time comes? That's the issue for me. I have absolutely no control over how I die, but I do have responsibility for how I go spiritually. God has given me the means of grace, the power of the Holy Spirit, and the truth of the Word to keep me on course. I want to look at my life the way Paul looked at his life—I want to finish well spiritually. Paul said, "It doesn't matter to me if I live or die. What matters is that faithfulness marks my life to the end." Having that perspective is one way to ensure you stay on course.

Fighting the Good Fight

Note particularly how Paul described his life of ministry: "I have fought the good fight." Recognizing that you are in a fight will help motivate you to finish well. In the original Greek text, "have fought" (*ēgōnismai*) and "fight" (*agōna*) speak of an intense struggle—it could be translated, "I have agonized the agony." Paul understood that this life is an ongoing, agonizing war that requires an immense amount of energy.

Many Christians assume that life should be easier as a believer, but it's not. It requires giving yourself as a sacrifice and placing yourself on the altar. It's a lifelong battle. So we shouldn't be surprised when things get difficult. In fact, we should worry when they aren't. A moment of peace is nice but it's also frightening, for that could mean there's a sneak attack coming up. It's always better to know where the battle is taking place.

Over my years of church ministry I've had people come up to me and say, "I hate to tell you this, but we have a problem over here." My response has always been, "You know what's worse than you telling me we've got a problem? Not knowing that the problem exists." That's because when we know about a problem, we can do something about it.

As long as Satan is active, we will be engaged in spiritual warfare. That's why we can expect the work of ministry to be hard, and it's going to take every effort we have to hang in there and endure. You cannot expect to go through life comfortably with everything going exactly the way you want it to. If you take that expectation into the ministry, you'll be a casualty because you can't wander in blissful ignorance in the middle of a battlefield without getting shot.

From the time Paul became a believer, he was at war. He fought against Satan, principalities, spiritual wickedness, Jewish and pagan attacks, fanaticism among the Thessalonians, incipient Gnosticism among the Ephesians and the Colossians, his own heart, his own disappointments, and on top of all of that he battled against his own flesh, which caused him to do what he didn't want to do. The Christian life is a never-ending battle. You can't ever take a rest; you can't ever let down your guard. Life is an ongoing spiritual struggle that demands supreme commitment and effort. And after all he had been through, Paul was able to declare, "I fought it all the way to the end."

Note that Paul called this fight "the good fight." Many of us consider ourselves to be patriotic and we enjoy hearing the national anthem. We are inspired by what the flag stands for and we feel the nobility behind it and our nation's history. That's also how we as Christians should feel every time we see a Bible. While we may be glad to take a stand for noble causes, our labor for God is the cause of all causes.

The word translated "good" in 2 Timothy 4:7 is the Greek word *kalon*— it means that the fight is noble, beautiful, profitable, excellent, delightful, and distinguished. I especially like the word *noble*. Paul was saying, "I fought a noble fight." It's the most noble of all fights—the fight for the honor of Jesus Christ, for the glory of the gospel, for the integrity of God's Word.

The men who come to the end of their life victoriously and are able to face the Lord with confidence are those who are faithful in the ministry God has called them to. They realize they are in a noble war, and they are fully committed to facing the battle head-on.

Finishing the Course

Paul then moved from the battlefield metaphor to a race metaphor—in 2 Timothy 4:7 he wrote, "I have finished the course." The word translated "course" is the Greek term *dramas*, which refers to an athletic race. Paul said, "I started the race, I ran it, I stayed on course, and I finished." He didn't run aimlessly. He stayed on the course and aimed for the finish line. He was focused and didn't waver.

This course Paul spoke of begins at conversion and ends in glory. He had begun the race on the road to Damascus and was soon going to cross the finish line. Along the way, he never lost sight of what God wanted him to do. The key to doing this is found in Hebrews 12:1-2: "Let us run with endurance the race that is set before us, fixing our eyes on Jesus, the author and perfecter of faith." Jesus was the model runner, and Paul followed after Him.

Have you ever run a race? I used to run sprints in my college days. I ran the 100 meter, the 200 meter, and occasionally the 400 meter races. I was rarely the winner, but I gave my best and my objective was to stay as close as possible to whoever was in the lead. Likewise, the winner of this spiritual race is Jesus Christ and right behind Him is Paul, and I'm endeavoring to stay with those two. They're my objective. This was the focus Paul had—one that reminds me of Rudyard Kipling's line:

> If you can talk with crowds and keep your virtue, or walk with kings and not lose the common touch, if neither foes nor loving friends can hurt you, if all men count with you but none too much; if you can fill the unforgiving minute with 60 seconds worth of distance run, yours is the earth and everything that's in it, and which is more you'll be a man, my son.[5]

The focused life is undisturbed by everything going on around you. Run the race well all the way to the end.

The apostle Paul also recognized the need to use his time well. If you're going to run the race so as to win it, then don't waste the time God has given you. In Ephesians 5:16, Paul wrote about "making the most of your time, because the days are evil." He was committed to running hard and fast so he could finish strong. What can you do to make Paul's epitaph your own? Follow his example!

Keeping the Faith

Paul saw life not only as a war and a race, but also as a stewardship: "I have kept the faith" (2 Timothy 4:7). The Lord put Paul into battle, and gave him a lane to run in and a trust to keep. Paul kept it faithfully. What was this trust? He had kept "the faith"—not a subjective faith, but the Christian faith, "the faith which was once for all handed down to the saints" (Jude 3). Paul was unwaveringly faithful to the Word of God.

**You have been given a sacred trust—
that of taking God's truth and making sure
it gets safely into the hands of the next generation.**

That should be the passion of your life as well. Not only are you a preacher of God's Word, you are also called to be its guardian. You have been given a sacred trust—that of taking God's truth and making sure it gets safely into the hands of the next generation. It's a guardianship for which you will answer to God. According to Hebrews 13:17, there will come a day when you have to give an account to God for what He entrusted to you. That's why you should become deeply grieved when you see people play fast and loose with Scripture, and it's why you should jump into the battle to defend God's Word whenever the need to do so arises.

In my preaching ministry, I am concerned that people take the Word of God seriously. I don't ever want to misinterpret Scripture, and I don't ever want to put words into God's mouth. People ask me, "Why do you study so much when you prepare your sermons?" It's because I want to get the passage right. I don't want to say, "God said" when He didn't say something. And I want to know how to protect God's Word from erroneous attacks. That is my stewardship.

What is my life? It's nothing but a sacrifice on an altar. The sacrifice is me giving up my life to fight God's battle, run His race, and keep His truth. That's what I'm called to do. I'm not reluctant about this calling, and I'm extremely grateful for it because it is the most noble of all callings.

The Crown of Paul's Life: Reward for Faithfulness

After Paul wrote about the past and present aspects of his life, he turned his attention to what was to come: "In the future there is laid up for me the crown of righteousness, which the Lord, the righteous Judge, will award to me on that day; and not only to me, but also to all who have loved His appearing" (2 Timothy 4:8). Isn't that amazing? When we go to heaven, the Lord will reward us.

What will we do with the crowns given to us? Cast them at Jesus' feet! Everything we do is possible only because of the glorious goodness of our Lord. Our righteousness comes from His righteousness, which He was able to give to us because Jesus Christ paid the penalty for all our sins. We're not able to fight the good fight, finish the course, and keep the faith on our own. It's all God's doing.

Note that Paul said this "crown of righteousness" was coming "not only to me, but also to all who have loved His appearing." What does that mean? Some might assume it refers to having an interest in prophecy, but that's not what Paul was talking about. Just because you read all sorts of books about Bible prophecy and you know every detail of what is to come doesn't mean that you love His appearing. There's nothing wrong with studying about the end times, but to love His appearing means having in your heart a longing for Jesus' second coming. If you can't wait for His return and you're saying, "Come, Lord Jesus," then that's testimony that you desire to be found faithful when He comes.

So look at your life like Paul did. Fast-forward to the end and ask yourself, "What will my epitaph be?" And this isn't just for pastors or ministry leaders; it's for every Christian. Wouldn't you like your epitaph to read like the apostle Paul's?

Maybe you're feeling discouraged because somewhere along the way, as you fought the good fight and you ran the race, you blew it. You let down your guard, you strayed from the course, you weren't a good steward of what God entrusted to you. If that's the case, don't think that means it's all over. God is a God of grace—Psalm 103:12 says, "As far as the east is from the west, so far has He removed our transgressions from us." So think of it this way: Today is the beginning of the rest of your life. From here onward, you will fight, you will run, and you will maintain the stewardship of God's truth. And when you're all done, the Lord will say, "Well done, good and faithful slave" (Matthew 25:23). And you will enter into the full reward that God has prepared for those who love Him.

PRAYER

Father, it brings joy to our hearts to know that You have prepared for us an eternal reward even though there are times when we fail You. Even Paul had times when he stumbled. But You have forgiven our sins, and we understand what You mean by faithfulness to the very end. You aren't talking about perfection, but faithfulness. May You find us always a faithful soldier, always a striving runner, always a careful steward of the treasure of Your truth to the very end. May it be true of us so that we can enter the fullness of the reward that You've prepared for all who love You. We pray in Your Son's name, Amen.

Bring the Book

"Ezra opened the book in the sight of all the people…
and when he opened it, all the people stood up."

Nehemiah 8:5

4

BRING THE BOOK

Steven J. Lawson
Shepherds' Conference 2006

Nehemiah 8:1-18

All the people gathered as one man at the square which
was in front of the Water Gate, and they asked Ezra
the scribe to bring the book of the law of Moses which the
LORD had given to Israel. Then Ezra the priest brought the law
before the assembly of men, women and all who could listen
with understanding, on the first day of the seventh month. He
read from it before the square which was in front of the Water
Gate from early morning until midday, in the presence of men
and women, those who could understand; and all the people
were attentive to the book of the law. Ezra the scribe stood at
a wooden podium which they had made for the purpose. And
beside him stood Mattithiah, Shema, Anaiah, Uriah, Hilkiah,
and Maaseiah on his right hand; and Pedaiah, Mishael, Malchijah, Hashum, Hashbaddanah, Zechariah and Meshullam
on his left hand. Ezra opened the book in the sight of all the
people for he was standing above all the people; and when he
opened it, all the people stood up. Then Ezra blessed the LORD
the great God. And all the people answered, "Amen, Amen!"
while lifting up their hands; then they bowed low and worshiped the LORD with their faces to the ground. Also Jeshua,
Bani, Sherebiah, Jamin, Akkub, Shabbethai, Hodiah, Maaseiah, Kelita, Azariah, Jozabad, Hanan, Pelaiah, the Levites,

explained the law to the people while the people remained in their place. They read from the book, from the law of God, translating to give the sense so that they understood the reading.

Then Nehemiah, who was the governor, and Ezra the priest and scribe, and the Levites who taught the people said to all the people, "This day is holy to the LORD your God; do not mourn or weep." For all the people were weeping when they heard the words of the law. Then he said to them, "Go, eat of the fat, drink of the sweet, and send portions to him who has nothing prepared; for this day is holy to our Lord. Do not be grieved, for the joy of the LORD is your strength." So the Levites calmed all the people, saying, "Be still, for the day is holy; do not be grieved." All the people went away to eat, to drink, to send portions and to celebrate a great festival, because they understood the words which had been made known to them.

Every great season of reformation in the church, and every great hour of spiritual awakening, has ushered in a recovery of biblical preaching. J.H. Merle d'Aubigne, the noted historian of the Reformation in Geneva and Europe, wrote, "The only true reformation is that which emanates from the Word of God."[1]

Such was certainly the case in sixteenth-century Europe, which witnessed the recovery of biblical preaching by men like Martin Luther, John Calvin, and John Knox. These Reformers turned the European continent upside down with their pulpit expositions. Such was the case in the golden Puritan era in the seventeenth century, which also witnessed the recovery of biblical preaching in Scotland and England under the likes of John Owen, Jeremiah Burroughs, Samuel Rutherford, Thomas Watson, and an entire army of biblical expositors. These Puritan divines shook the English monarchy with their bold, biblical preaching. Such was the case in the Great Awakening through the biblical preaching of Jonathan Edwards, George Whitefield, and Gilbert Tennent. These preachers took New England by storm and electrified the Atlantic seacoast with the preaching of the Word. Every great reformation, every great awakening, and every great revival has been ushered in by the recovery of biblical preaching. The noted church historian Phillip Schaff wrote:

> Every true progress in church history is conditioned by a new and deep study of the Scripture. While the humanists went back to the ancient classics and revived the spirit of Greek and Roman Paganism, the reformers went back to the Sacred Scriptures. In the original language, *ad fontes*, back to the fountain and revived the spirit of Apostolic Christianity. They were fired by an enthusiasm for the gospel, such as had not been seen since the days of Paul.[2]

Sola Scriptura and the preaching of the Scripture ushered in the Reformation. Describing that time, James Montgomery Boice wrote,

> Calvin had no weapon but the Bible. From the very first, his emphasis had been on Bible teaching. Calvin preached from the Bible every day and under the power of that preaching, the city began to be transformed. As the people of Geneva acquired knowledge of God's Word and were changed, the city became as John Knox said, "the most perfect school of Christ since the days of the Apostles."[3]

This is what is so desperately needed—a recovery not just of preaching, but of biblical preaching, expository preaching, and true preaching. That is why I love Nehemiah chapter 8—it puts its arms around what God has called you and me to do, which is to be expositors of the Word of God.

Here is the setting: the date is 445 BC and the place is Jerusalem. It has been less than one week since God's people rebuilt the wall around the city of Jerusalem under Nehemiah's leadership. It is a time in which the whole nation has come together to celebrate the Feast of Tabernacles. The temple has been restored and the city wall has been built. The people are back in the land after 70 years of captivity, but they need more than a mere building program and more than a crowd. They now need the preaching of God's Word to ignite their souls so that they may grow in the holiness with which God has called them to live.

In this passage, we examine a case for biblical preaching. In the first verse, Nehemiah presents the *cry* for biblical preaching. Then in verses 2 through 8, the *characteristics* of biblical preaching are delineated. Finally in verses 9 through 18, the *consequences* of biblical preaching are laid out.

The Cry for Biblical Preaching

The narrative begins where every revival and reformation must begin—with a cry and hunger for the preaching of the Word of God. In verse 1 the narrator wrote, "All the people gathered as one man at the square which was in front of the Water Gate." There were upwards of 42,000 people assembled by the water gate on the east side of Jerusalem near the Gihon Spring (Ezra 2:64).

Nehemiah 8:1 indicates that the people gathered as "one man," meaning they were intent on one purpose. They had come together for the right reason. They were there to make their plea, to cry out to their leaders to bring them the Word of God. Verse 1 continues, "And they asked Ezra the scribe to bring the book of the law of Moses which the Lord had given to Israel." This was remarkable. This plea came from the crowd—in a sense, from the pew. They were crying out, "Bring the Book! Bring the Book!"

Moses commanded in Deuteronomy 31:10-13 that the people of Israel were to come together every seven years for a corporate, public reading of God's Word. The Israelites had been in captivity for 70 years, and they were long overdue for this type of public gathering in the Holy City. They were eager to hear the Pentateuch read to them and the explanation to be given to them. They were under the heightened awareness of this reality and they cried out, "Bring the Book!" Ezra was the right man to step forward with the Book. It was 14 years earlier that Ezra himself had returned from captivity to Jerusalem to begin this ministry of teaching the Word. God had been preparing Ezra 14 years for this revival. He had been preparing the man for the moment, and the moment for the man.

A Singular Focus

No doubt you are familiar with Ezra 7:10: "Ezra had set his heart to study the law of the Lord and to practice it, and to teach His statutes and ordinances in Israel." This was Ezra's philosophy of ministry. He had "set his heart," which means that he was resolved and fixed. He was a man of one thing—he was a man of the Book. Notice the passage says that Ezra was "set…to study the law," which means he was ready to seek something through careful inquiry. This term carries the connotation of digging out, as a miner who digs out riches that are beneath the earth's surface.

Studying the truth is where any meaningful ministry begins.

This was the ministry to which God had called Ezra. He was a student of the Word. He had been doing this for at least 14 years leading up to this revival. Studying the truth is where any meaningful ministry begins. In 2 Timothy 2:15 Paul wrote, "Be diligent to present yourself approved to God as a workman who does need not to be ashamed, accurately handling the word of truth." The revival began with Ezra in front of an open scroll as he studied the Word of God. The man whom God calls into the ministry to be a preacher of the Word is supernaturally given an insatiable desire to study the Word of God.

I grew up in the home of an academician. My father was a professor in medical school. He was a brilliant man. Every morning, he rose early before I got up and was already off to the university. He had his laboratory. He did his research. He wrote his periodical articles. And he taught his classes. My brother is a professor at Vanderbilt Medical School, a cardiologist, and he too is a brilliant man. My mother was the valedictorian in her graduating class. My sister is an accomplished teacher. In contrast, while growing up, all I wanted to do was play football. When football season was over, I played on the basketball team. When basketball season was over, I played on the baseball team. While playing baseball, I also ran on the track team and lifted weights with the football team. During the summer I played golf, and in the fall my cycle repeated. That was my life. I did not want to study and I did not want to read.

During my senior year of high school, I signed a full scholarship to play football for Texas Tech University. When I signed that scholarship, I thought I would never have to study again. However, for my father, academia was the core value of being a Lawson. Right before I graduated from high school, my father sat me down and lectured me on the importance of academics, but I did not want to have anything to do with it. I went to Texas Tech and majored in finance, but ultimately I was there to play football. My whole life was immersed in athletics. I read CliffsNotes to pass classes and don't think that I even owned a book.

A couple years ago, my father visited my study at the church. The office walls were covered with books, and as my father stood in the middle of the room and looked around, he said, "Now I know there is a God in heaven. My son, the student." Then he walked over and hugged me. My father is a believer, and he rightly concluded that for me to become a student was a transformation only God could do in me. I had been primarily an athlete, but when God calls you into the ministry, He gives you an insatiable desire to dig into the text. It is a supernatural work of God, and if you do not have it, you have not been called. If God wants you to fly, He will give you wings. If God wants you to preach, He will give you a great hunger and desire for His Word. When He summons you, you will become a student of the Word. You will dig, dig, and dig into it, knowing that you must plunge into the depths of His inerrant, inspired, and infallible Word.

Ezra can be described with the same words that Charles Spurgeon used to describe John Bunyan: "Why, this man is a living Bible! Prick him anywhere—his blood is bibline, the very essence of the Bible flows from him."[4] Bunyan was a walking Bible, Ezra was a walking Bible, and you and I must be walking Bibles. We have nothing to say apart from the Word of the living God.

A Strenuous Pursuit

Not only did Ezra set his heart to study the Word, he was also determined "to practice it" (Ezra 7:10). He became a living epistle of what he was reading and learning. Ezra lived out the Word of God and put it into practice. This word "practice" is used elsewhere in the Old Testament and carries the idea of expending great energy in the pursuit of something. It's the word that was used to speak of Noah's strenuous effort in building the Ark. With diligent effort, Ezra was building the Word of God into his life. He was not passive in his sanctification. He was bringing his life under the authority of Scripture. He was striving to be an incarnation of the Book that he was reading.

A Strong Passion

In addition to studying and practicing God's Word, Ezra was committed to "teach[ing] His statutes and ordinances in Israel" (Ezra 7:10). This word "teach[ing]" indicates the image of instructing by goading and prodding, as a master would his ox. Not only was Ezra laying out information for those who were in front of him, but there was also a purpose to declaring the truth. He was pushing the people toward the will of God as he was teaching the truth.

This is what God has called us to be—students. We are to dig into the Word. Likewise, we are to be believers who live out the message. Moreover, we are to be preachers who teach it. The revival at the Water Gate began 14 years earlier when Ezra was alone with God, with the scrolls of Scripture unraveled before him, studying the Word, digging into the text, grasping its meaning, capturing its thunder, incorporating it into his soul, applying it in his life, and teaching it faithfully. This revival began with the people crying out for biblical preaching, and Ezra was prepared.

In like manner, the people in your congregation who truly know God and love Him are crying out to you in their hearts, "Preacher, bring the Book!" Sadly, there are pastors all over this country who instead of hearing the cry of their people are going to conferences where they are told, "Go out and survey unbelievers and give them what they want." If you go survey lost people, they are not going to say, "We want more Bible exposition." That is because "the natural man does not accept the things of the Spirit of God, for they are foolishness to him; and he cannot understand them, because they are spiritually appraised" (1 Corinthians 2:14). The unbelievers want entertainment and drama, and when we cave in to their carnal demands, we sin before the almighty God.

Yet among the faithful few, there is a cry for biblical preaching. Open your ears and you will hear it in your own congregation. This is the yearning that always precedes a great movement of God in reformation, awakening, and revival. Imitate Ezra's commitment to being a man who studies and digs in order to feed your people the Word of God.

The Characteristics of Biblical Preaching

As we build a case for biblical preaching, it is helpful to look at the characteristics of biblical preaching. Martyn Lloyd-Jones wrote, "What is it that always heralds the dawn of a reformation or of a revival? It is a renewed preaching. Not only a new interest in preaching but a new kind of preaching."[5]

Ezra's preaching was a specific kind of preaching. As we examine it, I want to point out five indispensable characteristics of biblical preaching. These should form the paradigm for our sermon preparation and delivery.

A Biblical Reading

The first characteristic of biblical preaching is to maintain a reading of the Word of God. Nehemiah 8:3 tells us Ezra's starting point when he proclaimed the Book to God's people: "He read from it before the square, which was in front of the Water Gate." Ezra began his exposition with a simple reading of the Book because he knew that the Bible is living and active and sharper than a two-edged sword (see Hebrews 4:12). As Ezra spoke, he had passion in his voice. This was not a monotone mumbling of the Word. In the original Hebrew text, the word "read" is *kara*, which means "to cry out, to call aloud, to roar, to proclaim." In fact it is the word used in Jonah 3:2 when God said, "Arise, go to Nineveh the great city and *kara*." Proclaim! And that's what happened: "Jonah began to go through the city one day's walk; and he cried out [*kara*]" (verse 4).

When Paul instructed young Timothy, he said, "Until I come, give attention to the public reading of Scripture, to exhortation and teaching" (1 Timothy 4:13). This is how you begin the exposition of the Word of God—with a reading of the passage. Public reading of Scripture is in keeping with Jesus' own practice. In the Gospel of Luke, Jesus entered a synagogue in Nazareth and took the scroll of Isaiah and read from it, then said, "Today this Scripture has been fulfilled in your hearing" (Luke 4:21).

Similarly, Paul challenged the Colossians to read Scripture aloud: "When this letter is read among you, have it also read in the church of the Laodiceans; and you, for your part read my letter that is coming from Laodicea" (Colossians 4:16). The pastor is to stand in front of the congregation and read the Word of God. In 1 Thessalonians 5:27 Paul said, "I adjure you by the Lord to have this letter read to all the brethren." John wrote in Revelation 1:3, "Blessed is he who reads and those who hear the words of the prophecy, and heed the things which are written in it."

This practice of a public reading of Scripture has long slipped away from the worship service. Yet it is the only part of the worship service that is perfect. When you do this, you are making these statements to everyone who is listening, that your sermon content originated from a specific text of Scripture. What God has to say is far more important than what any man has to say.

When you step into the pulpit, you are an ambassador of the King and you have arrived with His Book. You need to conduct yourself like a man of God. You need to be like Ezra and open the Bible and read from the text. When you read the Bible in preaching, you are making a statement to everyone who sits under you that you are a man who has nothing but the Word of God to bring to the hearts of people.

A Lengthy Treatment

The second characteristic of true biblical preaching is to present a lengthy treatment of the passage. Nehemiah 8:3 continues, "He read from it…from early morning until midday, in the presence of men and women, those who could understand; and all the people who were attentive to the book of the law." From sunrise to high noon, from 6:00 a.m. to 12:00 p.m., Ezra provided a full treatment of God's Word.

In order for there to be authentic Bible exposition, there has to be sufficient time for an introduction, transitions, homiletical points, and an explanation of the text. A genuine sermon involves word studies, cross-references, historical background, thematic context, authorial intent, application, illustration, exhortation, persuasion, and conclusion. Early in my pastoral ministry, one of the matriarchs in our church said, "Pastor, your sermons are becoming too long." I said, "Well ma'am, it all depends upon the size of the cup you bring to church. If you bring a little thimble to church, it will not take me long to fill it up. May God enlarge your heart for the things of His kingdom."

Sometimes I am asked to speak in a seminary chapel and the dean will say to me, "I want you to model Bible exposition. You have 22 minutes to preach." I cannot model Bible exposition in a compressed period of time—not true exposition of the Scripture. Ezra offered a lengthy treatment. Yes, there are variables you must consider when it comes to sermon length, such as your own giftedness and where your congregation is spiritually. Still, your responsibility is to provide a full disclosure of the truth.

An Authoritative Posture

The third characteristic of biblical preaching is an authoritative posture. In Nehemiah 8:4 we read, "Ezra the scribe stood at a wooden podium which they had made for the purpose." He is not sitting on a stool and casually sharing. He is not walking around gabbing. He is standing at a wooden pulpit, and the reason he is standing there is because the Word is opened before him. I become nervous when a pastor walks around the stage without a Bible in his hand. The preacher needs to be where the Bible is. If you are walking away from the pulpit, you better take the Bible with you because I am not going to listen to you without an open Bible in your hand.

Verse 4 also tells us Ezra's wooden podium was large enough to hold 14 people. Ezra mounted the platform in order to be seen and heard. He had six men on one side and seven men on the other. There was solidarity in this leadership team.

When the preacher is serious
about the Word of God,
it becomes contagious.

Nehemiah 8:5 goes on to say that "Ezra opened the book in the sight of all the people for he was standing above all the people." For Ezra to stand above the people was intentional. There was a transcendence about this moment. It was a way to indicate that God's message was not on their level. The message is coming down from above. Notice as well how the people reacted when Ezra opened the Book: "All the people stood up." When the preacher is serious about the Word of God, it becomes contagious. When you believe the Book and are ready to die for the Book, the people take notice. In Ezra's case, when he opened the Scriptures in front of all the people, they stood up. This is in response to the authoritative posture of the preacher.

It is worth noting the people's response to Jesus' preaching when He taught the Sermon on the Mount. Matthew said "the crowds were amazed at His teaching; for he was teaching them as one having authority" (7:28-29). Peter took a similar posture in his first sermon on the day of Pentecost when he stood up and said, "Men of Judea and all you who live in Jerusalem, let this be known to you and give heed to my words" (Acts 2:14).

There must always be an authoritative nature about the preaching of the Word of God. Martin Luther once said, "The pulpit is the throne for the Word of God."[6] It is from the throne of the pulpit that the Word of God is to reign. Phillip Brooks, in his famous 1877 preaching lecture series at Yale, said, "If you are afraid of men and a slave to their opinion, go and do something else. Go and make shoes to fit them. Go even and paint pictures, which you know are bad, but which suit their bad taste. But do not keep on all your life preaching sermons which say not what God sent you to declare."[7] The man who will preach the Word of God must understand that there is an authoritative nature to true biblical preaching.

A God-Exalting Thrust

The fourth characteristic of biblical preaching is a God-exalting thrust. In Nehemiah 8:6 we read that Ezra "blessed the Lord the great God." There seems to be an eclipse of the glory of God in the church today, but when Ezra brought the Book, he blessed the Lord and there was an unveiling of the glory of God. What happened in response? "All the people answered, 'Amen, Amen!' while lifting up their hands" (verse 6). The raising of the hands was emblematic of receiving the Word coming down from heaven.

The response to such a God-glorifying moment was that "they bowed low and worshiped the LORD with their faces to the ground" (Nehemiah 8:6).

The Lord was magnified, and the response was worship. This should be the effect of true expository preaching. When you are elevating God, you are lowering man. At the same time, you are magnifying the grace of God which spans that wide chasm. The more you lower God and the more you raise man, the more you trivialize the grace of God. But when you put God in His proper place, you put His grace on display.

A Faithful Explanation

A fifth characteristic of biblical preaching is faithful explanation. Ezra involved the Levites in his preaching. They were spread among the 42,000 people to help explain the Scriptures. It was like a relay—Ezra read the Word of God and they explained it. There is a proper emphasis on the mind in true biblical preaching, and we see this all through Nehemiah chapter 8. In verse 2 we read, "understanding"; in verse 3, "understanding"; in verse 7, "explained"; in verse 8, "understood"; in verse 12, "understood"; and in verse 13, "insight." The emphasis of all true Bible exposition is on a precise explanation of the text.

John MacArthur has said, "I like to say that the meaning of the Scripture is the Scripture. If you do not have the interpretation of the passage right, then you do not have the Word of God, because only the true meaning is the Word of God."[8] He continues,

> Authentic Christianity…is concerned first and foremost with truth. The Christian faith is not primarily about feelings, although deep feelings will surely result from the impact of truth on our hearts. It is not about human relationships, even though relationships are the main focus in many of today's evangelical pulpits. It is not about success and earthly blessings, no matter how much one might get that impression from watching the programs that dominate religious television these days. Biblical Christianity is all about truth. God's objective revelation (the Bible) interpreted rationally yields divine truth in perfectly sufficient measure…God wrote only

one book—the Bible. It contains all the truth by which He intended us to order our spiritual lives.[9]

This is Bible exposition. The preacher gives the authorial intent of the text and explains the text. He persuades with the text, exhorts with the text, and then moves to the next text.

As Ezra preached the text, the Levites explained it. Nehemiah 8:8 says, "They read from the book, from the law of God, translating to give the sense." This was necessary because (1) the Israelites had been exiled for many years in Babylon, so for some of them it was difficult to understand the Hebrew text, and (2) the foreign culture of Babylon had influenced the Jewish way of life, making it necessary to explain the meaning of God's Word. The Levites were going beyond mere translation and were explaining the text's meaning. This is at the heart of expository preaching. If you do not explain the text in order to let God speak through that text, you do not have expository preaching.

The Consequences of Biblical Preaching

When the Word of God is preached in the power of the Spirit of God, there is a powerful effect. Although the consequences are not always instant, God's Word does not return void (see Isaiah 55:11-12). Sometimes God calls us to labor faithfully for many years before we see results. I remind you that "the eyes of the LORD run to and fro throughout the earth that He may strongly support those whose heart is completely His" (2 Chronicles 16:9). God is looking for congregations and pulpits where His Word is given a fair hearing and His people are called to a complete commitment to it.

The Weeping of Repentance

In Nehemiah 8 we notice that the preaching of God's Word has an impact on the people: "Then Nehemiah, who was the governor, and Ezra the priest and scribe, and the Levites who taught the people said to all the people, 'This day is holy to the LORD, your God; do not mourn or weep.'" Why did he say that? Because "all the people were weeping when they heard the words of the law" (verse 9). The Word of God is a mirror that allows us to see ourselves for who we are. It enables us to see ourselves as God sees us. It removes our self-deception and allows us to see our sin and our need for grace. In this instance, as the Israelites came under this revelation, they began to weep and mourn.

George Whitefield was a prominent preacher whom God used mightily during the Great Awakening. On one occasion he preached to coal miners in Scotland. As Whitefield declared, "You must be born again," he noticed that their faces, which were covered with black soot, had white channels created by their trails of tears. These rough and vulgar men, after hearing the Word, came under conviction over their sins. The work of the Spirit, through the preaching of God's Word, pierces the hearts of men. It produces repentance and tears people down before it builds them up.

The Rejoicing of Restoration

Then after this repentance comes rejoicing. In Nehemiah 8:10, Ezra said to the people, "Go, eat of the fat, drink of the sweet, and send portions to him who has nothing prepared; for this day is holy to our Lord. Do not be grieved." Ezra no longer desired for the people to mourn; instead, he wanted them to realize that the joy of Lord was their strength. Ezra encouraged them by pointing them to the greatness of God, and a supernatural joy flooded their souls because their hearts had been cleansed through the ministry of God's Word. Verse 11 tells us, "The Levites calmed all the people, saying, 'Be still for the day is holy.'" The Word of God, when it is preached with power, brings a unique effect upon the souls of men.

That brings us to Nehemiah 8:12, where we see the apex of expository preaching: "All the people went away to eat, to drink, to send portions and to celebrate a great festival, because they understood the words which had been made known to them." Ezra's life of devotion to the Word of God preceded this moment for at least 14 years in Jerusalem, and the consequences were amazing. He had been digging and studying such that some say that he is the author of Psalm 119. Others say he memorized the entire Old Testament. What we do know with certainty is that Ezra was a man of the Word and a walking Bible. He stood up before the people of Israel and gave a proper instruction of the Word. As a result, the people were revived and transformed.

The Call

This is what God has called you to do. Do you hear the people who are crying in your church? The people who want to be fed and who desire for their souls to be nourished? Nehemiah 8 reveals for us the characteristics of biblical preaching and the consequences of biblical preaching. So bring the Book to your people.

In 1517, Martin Luther lit a match that ignited the fires of the Reformation that spread through the continent of Europe. Its flames soon leaped across the English Channel. Scotland and England were caught up in this Protestant movement, in which people were coming back to the fountain of the Scriptures. They asked Luther this question: "How did you bring about the Reformation? How did you turn Europe upside down?" He answered, "I simply taught, preached and wrote God's Word. Otherwise, I did nothing. When I slept, the Words so greatly weakened the papacy that never a prince or emperor inflicted so much damaged upon it. I did nothing. The Word did it all."[10]

Each of us has the same instrument in his hand. You are called by God to exposit it, to preach it, and to proclaim it. The more you study it, the more you live it, and the more you declare it, the more you will see this world change.

PRAYER

God, I pray that in this hour, in this place, You would raise up from this conference men who would be so committed to biblical preaching that they would literally storm the gates of hell. I pray that they would hold fast to sound doctrine, that they would give themselves to the deep study of the text, that they would be men of holiness and purity who would live the very message that they proclaim. As they step into the pulpit, may You be in the pulpit with them, to undergird them and strengthen them as they declare Your Word. Bring about another revival as You did in the days of Ezra. May it shake this country and shake every continent in the world. We pray this to the glory of Him who suffered, bled, and died for us upon the cross. In Jesus' name we pray, Amen.

Preaching and the Sovereignty of God

"He says to Moses, 'I will have mercy
on whom I have mercy,
and I will have compassion
on whom I have compassion.'"

Romans 9:15

5

PREACHING AND
THE SOVEREIGNTY OF GOD

R.C. Sproul
Shepherds' Conference 2004

Romans 9:10-16

Not only this, but there was Rebekah also, when she had conceived twins by one man, our father Isaac; for though the twins were not yet born and had not done anything good or bad, so that God's purpose according to His choice would stand, not because of works but because of Him who calls, it was said to her "The older shall serve the younger." Just as it is written, "Jacob I loved, but Esau I hated."

What shall we say then? There is no injustice with God, is there? May it never be! For He says to Moses, "I will have mercy on whom I have mercy, and I will have compassion on whom I have compassion." So then it does not depend on the man who wills or the man who runs, but on God who has mercy.

In the 1960s a friend of mine, John Guest, came to the United States from Liverpool, England. He came with a guitar slung over his back and had decided to give his life to a ministry of evangelism in the States. During his early weeks in America he spent time trying to familiarize himself with the country's culture and history. He visited Independence Hall, went and saw the Liberty Bell, and he visited the antique stores in the Germantown section of Philadelphia.

Many of these stores carry Revolutionary War memorabilia. As John went through them, he noticed placards that dated back to the eighteenth century which proclaimed, "Don't tread on me," and "No taxation without representation." He told me that in one of those stores he looked at a wall and a specific placard caught his eye—it said, "We serve no sovereign here." He said to me, "I was terrified when I read that—so much so, that I almost wanted to take the next ship back to England. I thought, *How can I possibly come to a people proclaiming the kingdom of God when they have a built-in allergy to sovereignty in their culture?*" I'll never forget the insight this stranger to our shores offered, for it was and is a fair assessment of our culture, even with regard to the evangelical church.

I do want to clarify that I've never met a professing Christian who would answer "No" to the question, "Do you believe in the sovereignty of God?" Every Christian I've ever asked has responded with a resounding, "Yes, of course I believe." What could be more axiomatic for a Christian to affirm than the sovereignty of God? We all understand that if God is not sovereign, He is not God. An affirmation of sovereignty is simply an affirmation of theism.

Now, even though people are quick to say, "Yes, I believe God is sovereign," I've discovered that if you scratch that affirmation just a bit—if you begin to probe it by asking two or three penetrating questions—you soon find out that the matter of God's sovereignty is a loosely held concept.

As a preacher of God's Word, I don't want you to be uncertain, but instead to be confident in and sure of God's sovereignty. To do that, there are three specific areas of sovereignty at which I would like to look. Although they do not exhaust the application of the sovereignty of God, they are a good place to begin.

God's Sovereignty over His Creation

The first area of sovereignty we need to discuss is with respect to our affirmation of God's control over His creation. God rules over nature, and He rules over history. This may seem elementary, but it is an aspect of God's sovereignty that is often overlooked.

> Part of the reason we make so many mistakes
> in our thinking about God is because
> we have been reared in a pagan culture.

As pastors, we're fragile and sometimes erroneous in our thinking. I'm sure that in my beliefs I have theological errors, and the response I receive to that statement is generally, "Why don't you get rid of them?" If I knew which ones they were, I would. Nevertheless, I affirm the things that I believe because I'm convinced that they are accurate. However, somewhere in that theology there will surely be some mixture of error.

I believe part of the reason we make so many mistakes in our thinking about God is because we have been reared in a pagan culture. Every single day we are bombarded by ideas that are pagan. From kindergarten to adulthood, in the movies we watch, in the novels we read, and in the television shows we observe our minds are being assailed with ideas, many of which get into our heads because we accept them without critical thinking.

Often we don't realize that some of the ideas we have been taught are antithetical to the Christian faith. When we are born again, we aren't instantly sanctified, nor do we suddenly have the mind of Christ. Instead, we have excess baggage that we carry through our Christian pilgrimage, and one of the most common notions that invades our thinking is a pagan view of nature.

Let me try to illustrate this: Imagine that I am holding a pair of glasses and I am going to throw them into the air and hope that I don't break them. What will make these glasses go up into the air, and why is it that they won't hover and stay in the air? Why is it that after they reach their apogee they will follow the law that says, "What goes up, must come down"? In a pagan view of nature, we say that what happened in this little experiment is that the glasses obeyed the fixed laws of a mechanistic universe—a universe whose physics operate according to inherent powers and forces. What will make these glasses go up is the exertion of energy and power from my wrist and arm, and what will make them come back down is the law of gravity, which is a force that is inherent in nature. If that's what you believe to be the case, you're thinking like a pagan.

God Is the Power Supply of the Universe

One of the most profound principles in the Word of God is a pronouncement the apostle Paul made in Athens on Mars Hill. Paul affirmed to the Athenians that "in Him we live and move and have our being" (Acts 17:28). After the Reformation, the theologians of the seventeenth century who were concerned about the way in which God relates to His universe and creation made a very important distinction in theology. The distinction was between primary and secondary causality. Primary causality represents the ultimate causal power for anything that takes place in the universe. Scripture universally affirms this power supply for all living and moving beings to be the sovereign power of the almighty God. Without that primary causal power, which rests in God, there can be no living, there can be no moving, and there can be no being.

At the same time, the Reformers understood that there are causal forces that are real and take place in nature. When I exercise my force to pick up the pair of glasses, I exert real force that produces a real causal action. I'm the one who moves, but the point is that I can't move my hand, I can't grab these glasses, I can't throw them into the air, let alone hope that they come back to the earth, apart from the sovereign power of the almighty God. But because of our pagan context, we adopt a view of a nature that operates independently from the sovereignty of God.

We must grasp the doctrine of providence. This doctrine was vividly displayed in the book of Genesis when Joseph confronted his brothers. Upon learning of his identity, they were terrified that Joseph, in his position of power, would exact revenge against them. But on the contrary he told them, "Do not be afraid, for am I in God's place? As for you, you meant evil against me, but God meant it for good in order to bring about this present result, to preserve many people alive" (Genesis 50:19-20). Joseph was saying that in this drama of history, there was more than one player on the stage. There were the actions, the causal power, and the intentionality of his brothers, but above and beyond their intentions was the ultimate forethought of God. Does not the Bible say the same thing with respect to the passion of Christ? Jesus was delivered into the hands of a mob by the determinant counsel of God (Acts 2:23).

This is not to say that human actions are inconsequential, but rather that they are secondary. Although secondary causes are real, we still need to make the distinction that there can be no secondary causality without the primary cause. You and I couldn't do a thing apart from the power of God. After the tragic events of September 11, 2001, the question I was often asked was, "Where was God on 9/11?" My response: "He's in the same place He was on 9/10 and on 9/12. He's the Lord God omnipotent who reigns and holds all of nature in His hand. He is the one who raises up nations and brings them down, and He rules over people and impersonal nature."

How Free Is My Free Will?

Another myth that is pervasive in our culture is the pagan view of human free will. How many times have you heard the dispute regarding divine sovereignty and human freedom or free will? I have heard people, including professing Christians, say, "God's sovereignty is limited by human freedom." Have you ever heard that? That's like me saying to my son when he was in sixth grade, "My authority ends where your will comes into play." Instead, I said to him, "Son, you have a free will and I have a free will; but mine is more free than yours." A person's freedom, which is real and true, is always and everywhere limited by the freedom of God. That's what we mean when we talk about sovereignty—God is the one who is sovereign, not us.

Proponents of Reformed theology do not deny human free will. I don't know of anyone in the history of Reformed theology who denies that even after the fall the faculty of the will remains intact and we are able to still make choices. However, fallen humans always choose according to their strongest inclination; they have the power to choose whatever they want. However, as Calvin is said to have stated, "If that's all we mean by free will, then free will is far too grandiose a term to apply to mortals."

The notion of free will that the world teaches us is that human beings are creatures who have equal power to do good and evil. However, this pagan view of free will is on a collision course with Bible's teaching that the fallen human will is enslaved to sin. We can still do what we want to do, but the problem is with the "want to." The Bible tells us over and over again that we don't want God in our thinking. We want to be sovereign, we want to be autonomous, we want to rule, we want to reign, and we want to do evil.

The Bible teaches that without Christ, we can do nothing. Martin Luther is said to have remarked on Jesus' words, "Apart from Me you can do nothing" (John 15:5) by saying that "nothing" is not "a little something." Jesus taught Nicodemus that unless he was born of the Holy Spirit, he could not even see the kingdom of God, let alone enter it (John 3:1-8). But there is this pervasive view, not only in the world but in the church, that unregenerate people can see the kingdom, can choose the kingdom, and can enter the kingdom all apart from God's sovereign work of grace in their souls. We must reject this notion and acknowledge that God is the primary cause of all things. As preachers, we must believe this and teach it.

God's Absolute Authority to Bind the Conscience

The second area of sovereignty we need to consider is God's absolute authority to bind the consciences of His creatures. God has the right to impose obligations upon us, and He can say to His creatures, "Thou shall, or thou shall not." We claim to believe this, but every time you and I sin, we challenge the truth of this proposition. When we disobey, we contradict the idea that God has the right to bind our consciences absolutely, for even in the slightest sin that we commit we are involved in an act of cosmic treason. Sin is the raising up of the human will and desire against the Lord God omnipotent and the rejection of His preceptive will.

It is surprising how quickly Christians strip God of His sovereignty when it comes to the matter of salvation. If Christians affirm the truth that God is sovereign over the universe and there's not a single maverick molecule running loose in His creation apart from His sovereign control, and if they affirm that God is sovereign in ruling over all people and their actions, then the next affirmation should be the sovereignty of God's grace in salvation. However, even when people agree that God is sovereign over creation, nature, history, and law, they still deny Him the exercise of His sovereignty when it comes to His purposes in salvation. It is this third area of God's sovereignty that I would like to examine in the rest of this chapter.

God's Sovereignty over Salvation

In Romans 9:10-16, Paul wrote about the purposes of God. After explaining the gospel, he wrote in verse 10, "Not only this, but there was Rebekah also, when she had conceived twins by one man, our father Isaac; for though the twins were not yet born and had not done anything good or bad…" Paul wanted his original recipients, as well as us, to understand that according to the purposes of God, there were two children who had the same parents, were in the same environment, lived in the same culture, and were even womb-mates. Paul belabored the point that prior to their birth, prior to their behavior, prior to their human decisions, and prior to their human actions, the purposes of God according to election already stood firm. God decreed that the elder would serve the younger (Romans 9:12).

Although Paul's affirmation was explicit, the popular view of election held in the culture and the church today attempts to soften the doctrine. But whether you like it or not, if you believe the Bible, you have to believe in some kind of doctrine of predestination because the term wasn't invented by Calvin, or Luther, or Augustine, it was the apostle Paul who used the language of election, choosing, and predestination. For example, in Ephesians 1:3-6 we read,

> Blessed be the God and Father of our Lord Jesus Christ, who has blessed us with every spiritual blessing in the heavenly places in Christ, just as He chose us in Him before the foundation of the world, that we would be holy and blameless before Him. In love He predestined us to adoption as sons through Jesus Christ to Himself, according to the kind intention of His will, to the praise of the glory of His grace, which He freely bestowed on us in the Beloved.

Therefore, if you're going to be biblical, you must affirm some view of the doctrine of predestination.

The Foreknowledge View of Predestination

The most popular view of this doctrine is a prescient or foreknowledge view that advocates that God looked down the corridor of time and saw who was going to make the right choice and on the basis of that choice He selected who would come to salvation. But this view doesn't explain the biblical doctrine of predestination, it denies it. I don't see how anyone can look seriously at what Paul taught in Romans chapter 9 and hold that position. Romans 9 is the most neglected text in all of Scripture by semi-Pelagians of all eras—they just don't want to deal with it. It was Romans 9 that brought me kicking and screaming into the Reformed understanding of predestination because Jonathan Edwards kept rubbing my nose in that text. I tried to get away from it with this logic: "Since the prescient view takes place before Jacob and Esau are born, I'm not denying that the decree of predestination took place before their birth; therefore, I can be an Arminian and still believe that part of the text." However, as we will see below, this logic was flawed.

In Romans 9:11-14 we read, "The twins were not yet born and had not done anything good or bad, so that God's purpose according to His choice would stand, not because of works, but because of Him who calls, it was said to her, 'The older will serve the younger.' Just as it is written, 'Jacob I loved, but Esau I hated.' What shall we say then? There is no injustice with God, is there?" In this passage, Paul was employing an ancient debating technique called *reductio ad absurdum*. Zeno of Elea, a fifth-century BC Greek philosopher, implemented this approach by standing in his opponent's shoes for a few moments, adopting the position of his opponent, and then taking that position to its logical conclusion, which revealed the absurdity of that position. In using this technique, the goal is to anticipate your opponent's objections and then state those objections in a more convincing and eloquent fashion than your opponent. After you've done that, then you dismantle that objection and reduce it to absurdity.

There was no greater master of this technique than the apostle Paul. For example, in 1 Corinthians chapter 15, in response to people who were denying the resurrection, Paul said, and I paraphrase, "Well let's look at the implications. If Christ was not raised, then what would that mean?" He then took that position to the point of absurdity in verses 13-19.

I used to teach pastors and lay people the same approach as we went through *Evangelism Explosion*.[1] We would go through the gospel presentation, and I would teach that when you get to a person's need for salvation, don't start by saying, "God is holy and God is a God of justice." Don't start there because the entire time you're telling a person that God is a God of justice, they are ready with their rebuttal, "God is a God of love." Therefore, start with that statement "God is a God of love," and talk about how incredible the love of God is and how marvelously the Bible communicates the idea that God is a God of love. Tell it better than the person has ever heard it, so then you can turn the corner and tell him or her that the same source that teaches about the love of God also teaches about His justice and that He will never clear the guilty. Then you're ready to discuss the cross. That is the technique the apostle Paul used in Romans 9:14.

After Paul introduced God's purpose according to election, he raised the question, "How do we respond to this, and what shall we say to this; is there unrighteousness with God?" I embraced the Reformed faith more than 40 years ago. Do you know how many times I have presented the case for the Reformed doctrine of election? And how many people have raised the objection, "That's not fair"? The objection is "If this doctrine is true, then it's not fair, and God is not righteous."

I don't think any Arminian in history has ever had to answer the objection. If you embrace Arminianism, you're teaching something that casts a shadow on the righteousness of God. Have you heard of any Arminian response to this objection? If you follow Arminianism, what could be fairer than for God to make the decision as to who gets saved when that decision is ultimately based on what people do? In Arminianism, if a person rejects the gospel, there is no notion of blaming God, for if the person's eternal destiny wasn't up to Him, it was the person's choice and therefore his or her fault.

Paul anticipated that some people would say, "That's not fair" in response to what he was teaching in Romans 9. At this point we're tracking with the apostle, for our view of election also provokes that response. Paul was anticipating the very objection that every semi-Pelagian in history has raised against an Augustinian understanding of grace: the false notion that there is unrighteousness in God if He elects only some people.

So how did Paul answer his own question? In Romans 9:14 he wrote, "What shall we say then? There is no injustice with God, is there?" Did Paul say, "Well, maybe," or "Sure looks like it here"? No, he gave the strongest negative response one can possibly give to a rhetorical question in the Greek language. Some translators render the original Greek text, "Certainly not!" Others put it this way: "God forbid!" To ask the question "Is there unrighteousness in God?" is to blaspheme, for there is no unrighteousness in God.

Paul elaborated on his argument by demonstrating that this teaching went back to Moses' writings. In Romans 9:14-15 he wrote, "May it never be! For He says to Moses, 'I will have mercy on whom I have mercy, and I will have compassion on whom I have compassion.'" Paul pointed to Moses to remind his readers that God's grace has always been sovereign. The Lord God Almighty is not bound by any law outside of Himself to dispense His grace to anyone; and if He gives it to one individual, He is not required to give it to another, He has absolute authority with regard to the granting of His executive clemency. God's sovereignty in salvation is not a New Covenant invention. Rather, it is an Old Covenant concept.

"That's Not Fair"

I would like to reinforce this truth with an illustration. Back in the 1960s I taught at a Christian college in New England. I was a Bible teacher, teaching the Old Testament, and my first class had 250 freshmen in it. The only classroom big enough to fit all the students was the chapel, so that's where we met.

On the first day of class I went over the syllabus for the course, and said, "You have three small papers due at various points throughout the semester. The first one is due September 30, and it must be on my desk by noon. The only exceptions to late papers are a death in the immediate family or if you're confined to the hospital."

I made the rules clear, and when September 30 came, 225 students turned in their term papers. The other 25 were trembling in their boots: "Professor Sproul, we didn't finish our papers; please don't give us an F for this assignment! Won't you give us a few more days to finish it? We haven't made the adjustment from high school to college, but we promise we'll never let it happen again."

I said, "You can have two days, but no more. Don't let it happen again."

October 30 came, and this time 200 students turned in their term papers and 50 did not. I said to the 50, "Where are your papers?"

The students said, "We had midterm exams, and it was homecoming week. We didn't prepare properly, and we didn't budget our time. Please don't fail us, Professor Sproul. Give us one more chance!"

I said, "All right. But this is the last time."

The students responded with overwhelming joy. In fact, they spontaneously broke out in song: "We love you Prof Sproul, oh yes we do!"

I was the most popular professor on the campus until November 30. On that date, 150 students turned in their term papers and 100 did not. I looked at the 100 and said, "Where are your term papers?"

They replied, "Hey, Prof, don't worry about it. We'll have them to you in a couple of days."

I said, "Johnson, where's your paper?"

He said, "I'm not done with it yet, but I'll get it to you."

I then took out every student's nightmare, the little black grade book. I said, "Johnson, you don't have your paper?"

He said, "No."

"Fine," I said, "that's an F. Harrison, where's your paper?"

He said, "I don't have it."

I made a mark in my grade book and said, "F."

With one voice a chorus of protests echoed through the chapel. Guess what the students said? "That's not fair!"

I said, "What did you say?"

They answered, "That's not fair."

I then looked at Johnson and said, "Did you say 'That's not fair'?"

"Yes sir."

"Okay, so it's justice that you want?"

"Yes," he said.

I continued, "Well, I remember that you were late with the last paper, weren't you?"

"Yes."

I said, "Okay, I'm going to erase last month's grade and give you an F for that one too."

Suddenly the room became quiet. No one mumbled another word.

"God forbid that I not be just." I declared. "Now, who else wants justice?"

After more silence, I said, "Maybe we should all sing the song, 'I've grown accustomed to His grace.'"

Amazing Grace

You see, when we experience God's grace once, we're grateful. When we experience it a second time, we become a bit jaded. By the third time, not only do we expect God's grace, but we demand it. We harbor in our souls the idea that if God doesn't choose us, there's something wrong with Him rather than with us.

The minute you get the idea that God is obliged to show His grace to you, you're no longer thinking about grace.

In Romans 9, Paul reminds us that God reserves to Himself the absolute sovereign right to pardon whom He will and to give justice to whom He will. Not one person in this universe deserves the grace of God. The minute you get the idea that God is obliged to show His grace to you, you're no longer thinking about grace. Grace, by definition, is something God is not required to give. That's the mystery of election.

One question many students ask me is this: "Why doesn't God give all people equal grace? Why isn't He an equal opportunity redeemer?" But that's the wrong question. The question every Christian should ask is, "Why me? Why did God bring me out of darkness and into light?" Think of your own conversion, and how God, in His grace, rescued you by His mercy and compassion, by a grace that is sovereign. "Hallelujah" should be your response.

The sad reality is that we sing "Amazing Grace," but we're not amazed by it. We must not only be amazed by grace, but we must be continually astonished by it. I still can't get over the fact that God chose me. One thing I know is that He didn't choose me because of anything He saw in me. God's choosing me was a gift to His Son so that the Son could see the travail of His soul and be satisfied (Isaiah 53:11).

This is the message we need to preach with regard to the passion of Christ; it was impossible that Christ could go through His sufferings to no avail. The idea that Christ came into the world to die on the cross to make salvation "possible" is blasphemous. He came into this world to make salvation absolutely certain for those whom the Father had given Him from the foundation of the world.

God's sovereign grace is love that is unfathomable. That's why when the apostle Paul talked about this doctrine of grace he broke out into doxology. In Romans 11:33 he wrote, "Oh, the depth of the riches both of the wisdom and knowledge of God! How unsearchable are His judgments and unfathomable His ways!"

As preachers, we must believe, teach, and find comfort in God's sovereignty over creation, history, our lives, our deaths, the salvation of our souls, and the salvation of the souls of those to whom we preach. May you preach and trust that God is sovereign to save.

PRAYER

Our Father and God, please forgive us when we presume upon Your grace. Let us always remember that we are saved by grace, through faith, and even that faith is not of ourselves, but is of You. So that salvation is not of him who decides, nor of him who runs, nor of him who wills, but of Thee who shows us mercy. Amen.

Has Any People Heard the Voice of God Speaking…and Survived?

"Know therefore today, and take it to
your heart, that the Lord,
He is God in heaven above and on the
earth below; there is no other."

Deuteronomy 4:39

6

HAS ANY PEOPLE HEARD THE VOICE OF GOD SPEAKING...AND SURVIVED?

Albert Mohler Jr.
Shepherds' Conference 2008

Deuteronomy 4:32-40

What an honor it is to be here among you men. As I stand in Pastor MacArthur's pulpit, I think about how many people have been affected by messages declared from this very location. I suppose there is no time when his voice is not being heard somewhere around the world, and it is John MacArthur's faithful example we are drawn to.

I've spoken to several pastors at this conference and have heard that some of you make it through the year in order to get here once again. I know that as I look out at you, I'm looking at preachers who find tremendous encouragement by being here in the company of other preachers. There is something precious and sweet about this conference and there is nothing else quite like it. This is one of the few places where you don't have to explain what you do for a living. It's one of the few places where you don't have to defend preaching. It's one of the few places where when individuals find out that you're a preacher, their faces light up. And it's one of the few places where you can come and make so many friends of fellow preachers.

The Task At Hand

There's no doubt that we are living in strange times. One of the hallmarks of our generation is the fact that there is a crisis in preaching. It would be an exercise of mass delusion if we were to act like there isn't a problem in our midst. Let me ask you a question in order to diagnose this current epoch: How likely is one to hear an expository sermon if he were to take a seat in an evangelical church? A candid answer to this question indicates that you really do not have the assured expectation that most evangelical churches practice the exposition of God's Word.

Do you believe that as time moves forward, it's becoming more likely or less likely for people to hear an expository message? To help you answer this question, look at the preaching literature published in the Christian world. Look at the resources available at popular conferences and seminars, and you'll see how little exposition there is. But by God's grace this is not true everywhere, and it's not true here among us—yet it is increasingly true in the church at large.

Once we diagnose this crisis and recognize that it exists, we have to ask why it's happened. It's almost as if by some form of strategy there has been a unilateral disarmament of the evangelical church when it comes to expository preaching. The exposition of the Scriptures should be the easiest thing in the world to understand. As a matter of fact, you have to be clever to mess it up. In Nehemiah 8:1-8 we see a display of what preaching is all about:

> All the people gathered as one man at the square which was in front of the Water Gate, and they asked Ezra the scribe to bring the book of the law of Moses which the LORD had given to Israel. Then Ezra the priest brought the law before the assembly of men, women and all who could listen with understanding, on the first day of the seventh month. He read from it before the square which was in front of the Water Gate from early morning until midday, in the presence of men and women, those who could understand; and all the people were attentive to the book of the law.

Ezra the scribe stood at a wooden podium which they had made for the purpose. And beside him stood Mattithiah, Shema, Anaiah, Uriah, Hilkiah, and Maaseiah on his right hand; and Pedaiah, Mishael, Malchijah, Hashum, Hashbadda-nah, Zechariah and Meshullam on his left hand. Ezra opened the book in the sight of all the people for he was standing above all the people; and when he opened it, all the people stood up. Then Ezra blessed the LORD the great God. And all the people answered, "Amen, Amen!" while lifting up their hands; then they bowed low and worshiped the LORD with their faces to the ground.

Also Jeshua, Bani, Sherebiah, Jamin, Akkub, Shabbethai, Hodiah, Maaseiah, Kelita, Azariah, Jozabad, Hanan, Pelaiah, the Levites, explained the law to the people while the people remained in their place. They read from the book, from the law of God, translating to give the sense so that they understood the reading.

Now, I didn't say that the exposition of Scripture was an easy task to do, but rather that it was straightforward and simple to understand. We see that "they read from the book, from the law of God, translating," or explaining, "to give the sense so that they understood the reading" (8:8). How is it possible to misunderstand that? What is it in the Book that we are capable of misunderstanding? The task at hand is simple: You read the Book and you explain it.

Simple Instructions

I want you to note carefully the expository pattern. This is not a scene from "the Ezra code." There's nothing hidden here. As an expositor, you are called to read and explain—that's fairly simple, isn't it? I heard some-one the other day say that there's still a fellow locked in the shower some-where because the instructions on the shampoo say, "Lather, rinse, repeat." Likewise, exposition is all about reading the text, explaining the text, going home, coming back, and again reading and explaining the text.

I recognize that instructions are often inadequate. I'm the kind of person who goes to a department store, buys a bicycle, and pays the store to put it together. I simply don't have the patience to struggle through the mistranslations of the English language into which the instructions have been written. A friend of mine, and his wife, when they were expecting their first child, went out to buy a crib. The father, in a moment of absolute commitment, said, "Tonight, I will put this crib together." And he did. There was only one problem—after a few hours of putting it together, he realized the instructions lacked a key bit of information: "Assemble the crib in the room where it will be used." He had to completely dismantle the crib, move it into the baby's room, and put it all together again.

Instructions can be confusing or inadequate, but when it comes to expository preaching the directions are clear: You are to read the Book and explain it.

Of course there is a bit more to preaching in terms of background. Scripture tells us that the messenger must be called. We read this in Ezra 7:6: "This Ezra went up from Babylon, and he was a scribe skilled in the law of Moses, which the LORD God of Israel had given; and the king granted him all he requested because the hand of the LORD his God was upon him." It isn't just anyone who is assigned to take up the instructions and fulfill the command. The hand of the Lord falls upon certain men who are called to preach. We need to recognize that calling is important and indispensable.

How do we know when a man is called to this task? We observe in Ezra 7:10 that Ezra was the man for the job because "Ezra had set his heart to study the law of the LORD and to practice it, and to teach His statutes and ordinances in Israel." Along with calling, studying was very much a part of what made Ezra a preacher. Ezra is described as being "learned in the words of the commandments of the LORD and His statutes to Israel" (verse 11). A preacher is one whom God has called and one whom the congregation recognizes that the hand of the Lord is upon him; and his response to this call is demonstrated by his preparation and his dedication to study, all of which is done in order to become skilled in the Word of God.

We have instruction in the New Testament as well. In 2 Timothy 4:1-2 the apostle Paul, delivering his final message to Timothy, sets forth that greatest priority of the pastoral calling, which is the preaching of the Word of God: "I solemnly charge you in the presence of God and of Christ Jesus, who is to judge the living and the dead, and by His appearing, and His kingdom: preach the word; be ready in season and out of season; reprove, rebuke, exhort, with great patience and instruction." I ask you again: How clever do you have to be to understand this? Paul used straightforward words and there aren't many polysyllabic constructions in this verse. The command is to preach the Word in season and out of season, reprove, rebuke, exhort, and patiently teach. This is the pattern.

If you're not reading the text and explaining, reproving, rebuking, exhorting, and patiently teaching, then you're not preaching.

Why is it not happening? Why is it that the exposition of the Scriptures is evacuated from so many of our churches, missing from so many of our pulpits, and alien to so many preachers? I understand preaching takes place all across the world, but is it expository preaching? According to the Bible, exposition is preaching. According to the Bible, if it isn't exposition, it isn't preaching.

You may call it a sermon, you may be called a preacher, and what you do may be called preaching, but if you're not reading the text and explaining, reproving, rebuking, exhorting, and patiently teaching, then you're not preaching. We have to stop saying, "I prefer expository preaching," and just say, "I'm a preacher. I read the text, explain it, go home and study it, and I come back and do it again." It's so simple, yet it's so tragically absent.

The Theology Behind the Instructions

The essence of the problem is not faulty technique but faulty theology. Since this problem is deeply theological, I want us to focus our thoughts on Deuteronomy chapter 4. I want us to think together about a theology of expository preaching, I want us to see what is at stake, I want us to see a means of recovery, and I want us to feel the urgency of this text as it applies to the exposition of the Word of God. Read with me Deuteronomy 4:32-40:

> Indeed, ask now concerning the former days which were before you, since the day that God created man on the earth, and inquire from one end of the heavens to the other. Has anything been done like this great thing, or has anything been heard like it? Has any people heard the voice of God speaking from the midst of the fire, as you have heard it, and survived? Or has a god tried to go to take for himself a nation from within another nation by trials, by signs and wonders and by war and by a mighty hand and by an outstretched arm and by great terrors, as the LORD your God did for you in Egypt before your eyes? To you it was shown that you might know that the LORD, He is God; there is no other besides Him. Out of the heavens He let you hear His voice to discipline you; and on earth He let you see His great fire, and you heard His words from the midst of the fire. Because He loved your fathers, therefore He chose their descendants after them. And He personally brought you from Egypt by His great power, driving out from before you nations greater and mightier than you, to bring you in and to give you their land for an inheritance, as it is today.
>
> Know therefore today, and take it to your heart, that the LORD, He is God in heaven above and on the earth below; there is no other. So you shall keep His statutes and His commandments which I am giving you today, that it may go well with you and with your children after you, and that you may live long on the land which the LORD your God is giving you for all time.

When you read the first-person singular in this passage, it is God speaking through Moses, and then Moses providing a commentary and reflection on what God has done and said. Deuteronomy is so intentionally theological that scholars of the Old Testament identify what they call the Deuteronomic Theology. It is the book of the Pentateuch that Jesus quotes from most often. And it is the third-most-quoted Old Testament book in the New Testament, next to Psalms and Isaiah.

The historical context of Deuteronomy is that the children of Israel are in the wilderness. Moses is preparing them to enter the Land of Promise. Behind them is the history of the Exodus, Sinai, and the rebellion at Kadesh Barnea. Before them is the River Jordan and on the other side of the river is the Land of Promise. This is the generation that will enter the land. But because the people will enter this land without Moses, the Lord is speaking to His people through Moses in order to prepare them for the challenges ahead.

The book of Deuteronomy is the second giving of the law. God has given His people the opportunity to be faithful rather than unfaithful and obedient rather than disobedient. How will they be readied and prepared? You'll notice that the book of Deuteronomy doesn't prepare the people with a military briefing, a demographic analysis, or a geography overview. Instead, the book concentrates on the Word of God. It's about the glorious truth that God has spoken. It's about the necessity and regularity with which God's people need to hear His voice. It's about the mandate to obey what God has said.

The theme of Deuteronomy chapter 4 is "hearken back to Horeb." After three chapters of introduction, the intensity of the text is raised in chapter 4 with the first words being "Now, oh Israel" (verse 1). In the Old Testament, especially in the book of Deuteronomy, this phrase is similar to the New Testament word "therefore," which aims to link future information with previous instruction. In other words, on the basis of what has been said in the first three chapters, the people must now be prepared to hear what follows. In Deuteronomy 4:1 Moses charges Israel to "listen"— listen to God because hearing His word is not a matter of success, but a matter of survival, life, and death. The entire theology of Deuteronomy comes down to the fact that God has spoken. Hearing and obeying is life, while disobeying is death. Moses wants the children of Israel to know that life and death hang in the balance of the Word. The pattern of the book is this: hear, listen, obey, and you will live. Refuse to listen and disobey, and you will perish.

I would submit to you that perhaps the central problem in our crisis of preaching is that somehow we believe this pattern has changed. Somehow we believe that God's Word was a matter of life and death in the wilderness, but it's a matter of something less in our churches. The only diagnosis I can offer of why expositional preaching is in decline, if not absent from so many pulpits, is the absence of the belief that the Word of God comes as a matter of life and death. But the truth is that it is *always* a matter of life and death, and woe to the preacher who forgets this truth.

With that in mind, in the rest of the chapter we will make four observations regarding the Deuteronomic pattern of preaching.

The Pattern of Preaching

The God Who Speaks

The first observation on preaching from Deuteronomy is that the true and living God is the God who speaks. We know who God is not because we were smart enough to figure Him out or because we were clever enough to entice Him into revealing Himself, but because out of His own love, grace, and mercy, He has spoken to us. The true and living God is the God who speaks.

Back in the 1970s, Francis Schaeffer wrote a powerful book titled *He Is There and He Is Not Silent.*[1] That book made a significant impression on my life because those two assertions actually frame the beginning of all Christian theology, of any Christian worldview, and of any understanding of who God is and what He would expect of us. We preach because He is not silent. What is the confidence in our preaching? Our confidence is that out of His Word, which is living and active and sharper than any two-edged sword, He still speaks. This is the miracle of revelation that I fear we give inadequate attention to in our churches, in our teaching, and in our preaching. God manifests His love for us in actually speaking to us, and in Deuteronomy 4:10-19 Moses makes this very clear:

> Remember the day you stood before the LORD your God at Horeb, when the LORD said to me, "Assemble the people to Me, that I may let them hear My words so they may learn to fear Me all the days they live on the earth, and that they may teach their

children." You came near and stood at the foot of the mountain, and the mountain burned with fire to the very heart of the heavens: darkness, cloud and thick gloom. Then the Lord spoke to you from the midst of the fire; you heard the sound of words, but you saw no form—only a voice. So He declared to you His covenant which He commanded you to perform, that is, the Ten Commandments; and He wrote them on two tablets of stone. The Lord commanded me at that time to teach you statutes and judgments, that you might perform them in the land where you are going over to possess it.

So watch yourselves carefully, since you did not see any form on the day the Lord spoke to you at Horeb from the midst of the fire, so that you do not act corruptly and make a graven image for yourselves in the form of any figure, the likeness of male or female, the likeness of any animal that is on the earth, the likeness of any winged bird that flies in the sky, the likeness of anything that creeps on the ground, the likeness of any fish that is in the water below the earth.

And beware not to lift up your eyes to heaven and see the sun and the moon and the stars, all the host of heaven, and be drawn away and worship them and serve them, those which the Lord your God has allotted to all the peoples under the whole heaven.

Moses declared, "Remember when you were there at Horeb? Remember when you heard the voice of God speaking from the midst of the fire?" What's interesting is that many of those who were listening to Moses speak were not at present at Horeb, and yet he tells them that they heard the voice of God. They were not there physically because many of them were not yet born, but they are under the Word just as their fathers and their forefathers were.

Moses stresses that they heard the voice of God. To prevent any confusion, he continues, "You heard the sound of words, but you saw no form—only a voice" (Deuteronomy 4:12). The context here makes it clear that the great danger is always idolatry. We have not progressed beyond Old

Testament idolatry; we've just become more sophisticated in it. The issue is always idolatry because in our fallen state we would rather have an image than a word. We would rather have an image we can control, because we can put an idol over here, dress it, and speak to it. This is the major distinction between the one true God and the false gods in the Old Testament—while the pagans speak to the idols, the one true and living God, who has no form, speaks to His people.

Elijah referenced this distinction when he confronted the pagan priests at Mount Carmel. In 1 Kings 18:29, we read, "When midday was past, they raved until the time of the offering of the evening sacrifice; but there was no voice, no one answered, and no one paid attention." Just think about those haunting words for a moment, and consider where we would be if God had not spoken. We would be in the same predicament as those pagan priests. We could do whatever we want, we could light whatever fire we want to light, we could come up with whatever creative message we desired, we could draw a crowd, we could even call it a church; but if God has not spoken, we are just as damned, dead, and lost as those priests.

Jeremiah spoke of idols in the same manner as Elijah when he said, "Like a scarecrow in a cucumber field are they [idols], and they cannot speak" (Jeremiah 10:5). It comes down to this: You either have the Word of God or a scarecrow in a cucumber field. It's either the God who speaks or it's an idol. Paul, in 1 Corinthians 12:2, wrote, "You know that when you were pagans, you were led astray to the mute idols." Now, Paul's challenge to remember is very different from Moses' challenge to the Israelites to remember. Paul asked the Gentile Christians in Corinth to remember that they were led astray and worshipped idols that don't speak, while Moses asked the children of Israel to recall when God spoke. In both instances, the emphasis is on the one God who speaks and reveals himself.

Revelation can be defined in this way: "Revelation is God's gracious self-disclosure, whereby He forfeited His own personal privacy, that His creatures would know Him."[2] The God who needs nothing, who is sovereign in His majesty and infinite in His perfections, forfeited His own personal privacy that we might know Him. Wouldn't you assume that the recipients of that revelation would live by it, be nourished by it, and cling to it? Wouldn't the natural response of those who are called to preach that Word be to read it and explain it?

Paul's reminder in Romans is similar—God reveals Himself to all the peoples everywhere through general revelation. There isn't an atom or a molecule in all of creation that doesn't cry out the majesty of the Creator. There isn't a single human being, made in the image of God, who does not have a conscience that cries out the knowledge of a Creator, and beyond that, the moral sensibility that one has violated His divine law. Paul also makes clear in Romans that mankind's problem is perpetual idolatry. The consequence of the fall is that there is not a single human being who by general revelation is going to come to a saving knowledge of the Lord Jesus Christ. This is where we are absolutely dependent not upon general revelation, but special revelation, which came in the form of a voice as God spoke.

However, if you think that God's speaking was all in the past, then resign from preaching. I say that with dead seriousness. If you do not believe that God now speaks from His Word, what do you think you're doing? Furthermore, if you do not have the confidence that God is speaking through you, insomuch as you rightly read and rightly explain the Word of God, then quit. We are completely dependent upon supernatural revelation, and as God spoke in times past, what we have now is the Scripture. This book we call the Bible is written, inspired, and God-breathed revelation. Through the Scriptures we have God speaking to His people now, even as He spoke to His people in times past.

The Bible is the inerrant and infallible Word of God, and if you believe that it's anything less than perfect, then you believe that even if God speaks, He speaks haltingly and falteringly. You believe that His voice is in there somewhere, rather than hearing it in every single word of Scripture. We must realize that God's voice is in every word, and just as "He spoke long ago to the fathers in the prophets in many portions and in many ways, in these last days has spoken to us in His Son" (Hebrews 1:1). His Word makes all the difference between true and false religion and between life and death.

What if God had not spoken? What if God had not called unto Moses from the burning bush, which was not consumed? What if God had not spoken to His children gathered there at Horeb? What if God had not spoken through the law? What if God had not spoken through the prophets? What if God had not spoken in these latter days through His Son? Then we would be lost in an aimless, meaningless, and nihilistic cosmos. If God has not spoken and if God does not speak now, then eat, drink, and be merry, for tomorrow you die. But God has spoken, and as a result, that message is a matter of life and death. That message is death to those who will not hear and life to those who do.

God's People Hear God Speak and Obey

The second observation on preaching from Deuteronomy is that God's true people are identified as those who hear God's words. The doctrine of revelation is essentially tied, not only in terms of epistemology and authority, to the doctrine of election. How do you recognize God's people? It's because He speaks to them. God did not speak to all the nations of the earth, but to Israel. He chose them from among the nations, and their election was confirmed by receiving revelation. Moses would remind Israel time and time again, "Remember that Yahweh didn't speak to everyone, but He spoke to you." The intent was not to produce an arrogant, self-confident people, but a nation who understood that it's only by grace and mercy that God chose to reveal Himself.

Chosen for God's Own Possession

In Deuteronomy 4:32-34, Moses asked a series of four questions to further support the truth that Israel was God's chosen people. The first question he asked was concerning the Exodus, the giving of the law, and the entirety of Israel's history. Had anything like these events occurred before? The answer, of course, is no.

Moses moved to the second question and asked, "Has anything been heard like it?" No other people could claim that they had a God who spoke to them, who did miracles for them, and who was creating in them a people for His own glory. Israel was alone among the nations to whom this had occurred—it hadn't even been rumored to have happened elsewhere.

The third question, in Deuteronomy 4:34, asked Israel if "a god tried to go to take for himself a nation from within another nation by trials, by signs and wonders and by war and by a mighty hand and by an outstretched arm and by great terrors, as the LORD your God did for you in Egypt before your eyes?" The world knew that Israel was God's chosen people and that they had been freed by God's hand from captivity and now existed for His good pleasure because of her redemption. This is similar to what is written in Joshua 4:6: "What do these stones mean to you?" The answer is in verse 7: "So these stones shall become a memorial to the sons of Israel forever." In the Old Testament, the people of God were constantly reminded that they were once captives to Pharaoh and Egypt but God Almighty had freed them by His mighty hand.

The fourth and final question Moses asked is in Deuteronomy 4:33, which becomes the primary focus of our discussion. It's one of the sweetest, most powerful, most incredible questions asked anywhere in Scripture. God, speaking through Moses, asked the children of Israel, "Has any people heard the voice of God speaking from the midst of the fire, as you have heard it, and survived?" How do the people of Israel know that they are God's people? How do they know that God has chosen them and that they are His? Because no other people had heard the voice of the transcendent, almighty, sovereign, omniscient, and omnipotent God speak from the fire and survived. If He just uttered His voice to us we would be annihilated, but instead He lowers His voice and He speaks to us as a Father to His children. Israel was there at Mount Horeb and the Lord God almighty spoke as a Father to His children so that they would live. These questions demonstrate that Israel came to know its privileged position, calling, election, and place in God's plan of salvation.

This level of privilege with regard to receiving the revelation of God is not just an Old Testament reality; it is also found in the New Testament. In Matthew 13:11, Jesus said to the disciples, "To you it has been granted to know the mysteries of the kingdom of heaven, but to them it has not been granted." This privilege was bestowed on the disciples not because of their intelligence, giftedness, or personality, but because God's sovereignty determined to glorify Himself through them. Jesus said to His disciples that the way you know you are Mine is because "to you it has been granted to know the mysteries of the kingdom of heaven, but to them it has not been granted." Jesus continued, "Blessed are your eyes, because they see; and your ears, because they hear. For truly, I say to you that many prophets and righteous men desired to see what you see, and did not see it, and to hear what you hear, and did not hear it" (Matthew 13:16-17).

Chosen to Testify

For the modern-day reader, how do you know that you're a believer in the Lord Jesus Christ? To answer that question, let me ask you two qualifying questions. How do you explain why you're a believer? We are saved by grace through the hearing of His marvelous message of salvation: "Blessed are your ears for they hear, and your eyes for they see. It has been granted to you to know the mysteries of the kingdom of heaven, but to them it has not been granted." This is no different than God saying to Israel, "I'm speaking to you as My chosen people. Out of all the nations, I am picking you." It's not about Israel's power, glory, wisdom, talents, or potential. God chose this tiny people group who couldn't even draw a straight line through the wilderness in order to show His glory as the redeeming, saving God who is faithful to His promises.

The reason is the same for why God chose us and allowed us to hear His revelation. Paul told the Corinthians, "God has chosen the foolish things of the world to shame the wise, and God has chosen the weak things of the world to shame the things which are strong" (1 Corinthians 1:27). It's because of the grace and mercy of God. This must produce humility and not arrogance and it should lead to witness—"So keep and do them, for that is your wisdom and your understanding in the sight of the peoples who will hear all these statutes and say, 'Surely this great nation is a wise and understanding people'" (Deuteronomy 4:6-8). God's special revelation was not just about Israel even as it's never just about us.

This kind of testimony will lead the nations to ask the following question: "What great nation is there that has a god so near to it as is the LORD our God whenever we call on Him?" (Deuteronomy 4:7). And furthermore, "What great nation is there that has statutes and judgments as righteous as this whole law which I am setting before you today?" (Deuteronomy 4:8). With these two response questions God was saying, "Israel, it's not about you. It's about what I'm going to do through you. When My covenant with you is made clear and you obey Me and follow My statutes, the other nations of the earth are going to say, 'What in the world is going on there? What nation has a God so gracious as to give this people such just laws? What nation is this that has heard from the one true and living God, and yet survives?'" In all of this revelation, God's sovereign purpose is to create a people by saving them with the blood of His Son for His own glory. We are identified by the same mercy that Israel received—we've heard Him speak.

God's People Survive by Hearing God's Word

The third observation about preaching we can make from Deuteronomy is that God's people survive by hearing His Word, for it is a matter of life and death. This observation is found in the concluding portion of the book of Deuteronomy. We read,

> This commandment which I command you today is not too difficult for you, nor is it out of reach. It is not in heaven, that you should say, 'Who will go up to heaven for us to get it for us and make us hear it, that we may observe it?' Nor is it beyond the sea, that you should say, 'Who will cross the sea for us to get it for us and make us hear it, that we may observe it?' But the word is very near you, in your mouth and in your heart, that you may observe it (30:11-14).

Moses communicated God's message that Israel did not find God's word by searching for it; it came to Israel and now it's very near to her. Similarly, the preacher finds answers that lead directly back to the Word of God. We have this Word, and this Word has consequences:

> See, I have set before you today life and prosperity, and death and adversity; in that I command you today to love the Lord your God, to walk in His ways and to keep His commandments and His statutes and His judgments, that you may live and multiply, and that the Lord your God may bless you in the land where you are entering to possess it. But if your heart turns away and you will not obey, but are drawn away and worship other gods and serve them, I declare to you today that you shall surely perish. You will not prolong your days in the

land where you are crossing the Jordan to enter it and possess it. I call heaven and earth to witness against you today, that I have set before you life and death, the blessing and the curse. So choose life in order that you may live, you and your descendants, by loving the LORD your God, by obeying His voice, and by holding fast to Him; for this is your life and the length of your days, that you may live in the land which the LORD swore to your fathers, to Abraham, Isaac, and Jacob, to give them (Deuteronomy 30:15-20).

For Israel, the Word was like manna. They had to have it fresh every day in order to survive. They lived as God's people by His Word and it became their help, blessing, and identity.

In 2 Timothy 3:16-17, Paul provided us with a similar and eloquent testimony of Scripture. He wrote, "All Scripture is inspired by God and profitable for teaching, for reproof, for correction, for training in righteousness; so that the man of God may be adequate, equipped for every good work." Nothing else is adequate except for the written revelation of God. Paul's testimony spoke not only to the authority, perfection, inerrancy, and infallibility of the Word of God, but also to its sufficiency, for it alone will accomplish these things.

We have to live by the Word, just as much as Israel had to live by the Word, for that's how we know who we are and who God is. It's in this Word that we find the testimony of Christ—He spoke of the perfect and enduring quality of Scripture in Matthew 5:17-18: "Do not think that I came to abolish the Law or the Prophets; I did not come to abolish but to fulfill. For truly I say to you, until heaven and earth pass away, not the smallest letter or stroke shall pass from the Law until all is accomplished."

How are we going to know who we are? How are we going to know we are His? How are we going to know how to live? How are we going to know the life-and-death issues of obedience and disobedience? How are we going to grow in grace? It is only through the ministry of the Word.

God-Honoring Preaching Is a Matter of Life and Death

The fourth and final observation about preaching we perceive from Deuteronomy is that it is always a matter of life and death. Since God's people survive by hearing God's Word, preaching must be the exposition of the Scriptures, because nothing else will do. Preaching is not merely about growing our churches, inspiring our people, or making people live more faithfully than before. God-honoring preaching is a matter of life and death. We either believe that or we don't. As Deuteronomy 30:19 says, "I have set before you life and death, the blessing and the curse. So choose life in order that you may live."

When it is the Word of God that speaks through the preacher, then it is God who speaks.

So Who Will Speak—the Preacher or God?

We have the Bible. If we know the Bible to be the perfect and God-breathed written Word, then we must view it in its proper perspective. It comes down to the question of who is going to speak: the preacher, or God? There are a whole lot of preachers doing a whole lot of speaking, but when it is the Word of God that speaks through the preacher, then it is God who speaks. That's the difference between life and death. Do we arrogantly think that God's redeemed people can live on our words? Or do we realize that life is found only in the Word of God?

We live only because He is there and He is not silent. Those who are called to preach are commissioned to study, stand before God's people, read the text, explain the text, reprove, rebuke, exhort, and patiently teach. We are called to keep doing this until Jesus comes or we die. Our hope and prayer in this endeavor is for our people, as they leave the church building, to turn and say to one another, "Did we really hear the voice of God speaking from the midst of the fire and survive?"

PRAYER

Our Father, I pray that You will raise up an army of expositors who will preach in season and out of season, through whom You will speak through Your Word. Father, may we have nothing to do with anything less or with anything other. May we see Your glory. May we see Your church recovered by preaching. May we see You bring glory to Your name as You honor Your Word. We pray this in the name of our Savior, the Lord Jesus Christ, Amen.

The Passion and Power of Apostolic Preaching

"It shall be that everyone who calls
on the name of the Lord will be saved."

Acts 2:21

7

THE PASSION AND POWER OF APOSTOLIC PREACHING

Steven J. Lawson
Shepherds' Conference 2007

Acts 2:14-24

I want to persuade you to be an expository preacher. I am not referring to just any kind of expositor, but a preacher who has the thunder of the apostles as they heralded and proclaimed the Word of the living God. The church does not need any more mild and meek preachers in pulpits. We need men of God to stand up, to speak up, and to herald the full counsel of God. We need the passion and the power of apostolic preaching to be upon our lives.

Two Dangers

As the church advances into the twenty-first century, I see two deadly dangers that concern me greatly—dangers that are threatening the very lifeblood of modern preaching.

The first threat is the devaluation of preaching in many churches. In this radical paradigm shift, biblical preaching is being displaced in favor of other alternatives. Exposition, once the main staple of the pulpit, is now being replaced with entertainment. Theology is giving way to theatrics. Sound doctrine is being exchanged for sound checks. The unfolding drama of redemption is becoming substituted for just plain drama.

God-exalting and soul-awakening preaching is out and casual dialogues are in. The straightforward exposition of Scripture is being demoted to secondary status.

This threat worries me, but it is not my greatest concern. The other danger lies entirely on the opposite end of the preaching spectrum. It is a threat far more subtle and one that endangers those who value biblical preaching. It is a stifling danger that is encroaching upon those whose exegesis is sound, whose study is deep, whose cross-references are dotted, and whose manuscripts are prepared. The problem is that their expository preaching is all exposition with no preaching. It is little more than a data dump. It is a lifeless lecture on the Bible. Their preaching has become clinical, cold, sterile, and stagnant. It is all light and no heat; it is precision without power. It is this second problem that most concerns me. Richard Baxter, the great Puritan minister, once said, "Nothing is more indecent than a dead preacher speaking to dead sinners, the living truth of the living God."[1]

R.C. Sproul has rightly said, "Dispassionate preaching is a lie, it denies the very content it conveys."[2] Walter Kaiser has weighed in on this and said, "Away with all the mediocre, lifeless, boring, lackluster orations offered as pitiful substitutes for the powerful Word of the living God. If that Word does not thrill the preacher and fill him with an intense desire to glorify God, how shall he ever expect it to have any effect upon his hearers?"[3] Martyn Lloyd-Jones has defined preaching as theology coming through a man who is on fire for God.[4] I believe that this is what must be recaptured among us who are called into ministry. We are not in danger of giving up the pulpit and inviting entertainment into our worship service. It is us, who believe in the authority of the Word of the living God, who all too often are lifeless in our exposition of the Scriptures.

We must look to the apostolic preaching that burst onto the scene in the first century. Every reader of Acts should be impressed with how dominant, powerful, and passionate apostolic preaching was. There are 19 major sermons or defenses of the faith in the book of Acts. It has been suggested that Acts could just as easily be entitled, "The Sermons of the Apostles." There are eight sermons by Peter, one sermon by Stephen, one by James, and nine sermons by Paul—five that are messages, and four that are defenses. Twenty-five percent of the book of Acts is devoted to recording the words of apostolic preaching in the early church. One out of every four verses in the book of Acts is a sermon or a defense of the faith. That underscores to us how important apostolic preaching was. It also suggests to us the kind of preaching that we are to emulate. One of the reasons these sermons are recorded in Acts is so that we might follow their timeless pattern in our preaching.

What Is Needed

It is not just expository preaching that we need, but expository preaching of a certain tone and with a certain thrust. What we need is apostolic expository preaching. We need to bring the thunder back into the pulpit. As we look in Acts chapter 2, I want to bring to your attention four marks of apostolic preaching that ought to direct every expositor who preaches the Word of God.

> This is the preacher's greatest glory—
> to set forth the majesty and supremacy
> of the Lord Jesus Christ.

First, preaching must be authoritative. Second, preaching must be text-driven. It must start with Scripture, continue with Scripture, stay with Scripture, and conclude with Scripture. The preacher never deviates nor departs from the central thrust of the Word of God. Third, preaching must be Christ-centered. It is a magnification and exaltation of the presentation of the person and work of Jesus Christ; this is the preacher's greatest glory—to set forth the majesty and supremacy of the Lord Jesus Christ. And fourth, preaching must be heart-piercing.

These four marks are found in the sermon Peter delivered on the day of Pentecost, and I suggest that as preachers we are to stand on the shoulders of the apostles and not only preach what they preached, but also preach as they preached. This will involve the following:

Preaching Must Be Authoritative

The first mark of apostolic preaching is that it is preaching with authority. As Peter stepped forward to preach, he did not offer suggestions to his listeners. He was not laying out mere options for them. On the contrary, Peter was assertive, emphatic, confident, commanding, directional, outspoken, and compelling. In fact, he was arrested for his preaching. Luke records this in Acts 2:14-24:

> Peter, taking his stand with the eleven, raised his voice and declared to them: "Men of Judea and all you who live in Jerusalem, let this be known to you and give heed to my words. For these men are not drunk, as you suppose, for it is only the third hour of the day; but this is what was spoken of through the prophet Joel: 'And it shall be in the last days,' God says, 'That I will pour forth of My Spirit on all mankind; and your sons and your daughters shall prophesy, and your young men shall see visions, and your old men shall dream dreams; even on My bondslaves, both men and women, I will in those days pour forth of My Spirit and they shall prophesy. And I will grant wonders in the sky above and signs on the earth below, blood, and fire, and vapor of smoke. The sun will be turned into darkness and the moon into blood, before the great and glorious day of the Lord shall come. And it shall be that everyone who calls on the name of the Lord will be saved.'"

As Peter stood before this crowd, his listeners had to decide which way they would go as a result of hearing his proclamation. Notice how the narrative begins in verse 14: "Peter, taking his stand with the eleven..." Peter took his stand as he stepped forward to preach. Luke's use of this verb translated "taking a stand" means far more than merely arising from a sitting position to stand on one's feet. What is being described here is Peter arising to take a firm stand and establish himself. John Calvin commented on Luke's description of Peter in this scene, saying, "He had something very serious to say and wanted to be heard."⁵ Peter assumed an authoritative posture by standing with the other apostles, who flanked him on both sides. Their presence added to the sense of Peter's authority as he declared the Word of God.

Luke also wrote in verse 14 that Peter "raised his voice." He was passionate, assertive, and sure. He had been trained by the Lord Jesus Christ himself. In John 7:37, it was Jesus who similarly expressed passion in His preaching when He taught at the Feast of the Tabernacles. John recorded that moment and wrote, "Jesus stood and cried out, saying, 'If anyone is thirsty, let Him come to me and drink.'" As Peter stepped forward and raised his voice, he did so as he had seen his Lord do so many times. This is not to say you need to be loud in order to be passionate, for there must be an ebb and flow in your volume as you speak the Word of God. Yet there must be a deep intensity conveyed.

I remember an incident in a class on preaching at Dallas Theological Seminary that highlights the importance of passion in preaching. In a preaching lab, a student was mumbling out his sermon as he preached to his fellow students. Professor Howard Hendricks interrupted his message in front of the class and said, "You do not believe that." The student responded, "Well I do." Hendricks said again, "Apparently, you do not." As this went on, the student became worked up and frustrated. He began to speak with deep conviction. Hendricks then said, "All right, get up there and preach it just like that. Let us know that you believe what you are saying. Once you convince us that you believe this, then maybe we will buy what you are selling." So it must be with every preacher.

Luke continued his description of Peter's sermon by noting his delivery: "Peter...declared to them" (Acts 2:14). Here Luke employed the term "declare" to describe the clarity of Peter's message. He was plainly heard and clearly understood. If there was to be a problem with those who were listening, it would not be because they had misunderstood Peter, but because they had heard exactly what he had to say. The word "declare" carries the idea of speaking seriously with gravitas. There was a gravity and a sobriety about Peter as he stepped forward to preach. He preached as if lives depended on it, as if souls were hanging in the balance.

Peter was confident and bold. There was no equivocation nor hesitation in his delivery. He said, "Men of Judea and all you who live in Jerusalem, let this be known to you" (verse 14). Peter spoke as a man who had been given a mandate by God and sent as the Lord's ambassador to be His mouthpiece upon the earth. Peter was not like those preachers who stroke their chin and say, "Well, it seems to me..." You do not want to listen to anyone who says that. You want to listen to a preacher who says, "Let this be known to you."

Peter then said, "Give heed to my words" (verse 14). He demanded that he be heard. He was saying, "Listen up, pay attention, and do not ignore me." That is the manner in which we are to stand up and preach God's Word. Peter then became corrective and showed his listeners the error of their ways when he said to them, "These men are not drunk, as you suppose, for it is only the third hour of the day" (verse 15). He reproved the crowd for wrongly assuming that the apostles were drunk.

Peter's authoritative approach continued through the rest of his sermon. In verse 22 he said, "Listen to these words." In verse 29 he asserted himself again when he said, "Brethren, I may confidently say." And finally in verse 36, he maintained certainty about his message: "Let all the house of Israel know for certain." The tone of Peter's entire sermon was characterized by authority and conviction.

Every gospel preacher and every true expositor must preach with the same authoritative boldness. We must speak the truth in love, but we must speak the truth. That is how Jesus taught and preached. At the very end of the Sermon on the Mount, "When Jesus had finished these words, the crowds were amazed at His teaching; for He was teaching them as one having authority, and not as their scribes" (Mathew 7:28-29). Where are the men who are marked by authority when they speak from the Word of the living God?

Paul taught Titus to preach in the same way: "These things speak and exhort and reprove *with all authority. Let no one disregard you*" (Titus 2:15, emphasis mine). This necessitates that our preaching be commanding and authoritative. Yes, we are to be kind, loving, patient, and long-suffering. But as we stand with the Word of God in our hand, we are to be exactly as

Peter was—we are to be bold, we are to raise our voice, we are to declare to our listeners, and we are to call for a verdict. In 1 Corinthians 16:13, Paul wrote, "Stand firm in the faith, act like men, be strong." Too many men are tripping over their skirts in the pulpits because there is a feminization of the pulpit today.

The problem with preachers today is that nobody wants to kill them. Peter was crucified. James was beheaded. Stephen was stoned to death. Paul was imprisoned and beheaded. All of the apostolic preachers died a martyr's death but one—John, who was held in confinement on the island of Patmos. The apostles were persecuted for what they believed and boldly declared. If there are people in your church who are in your ear urging you to tone it down, by the grace of the Holy Spirit do not listen to them. Instead, preach the full counsel of God in all that it says and affirms. That is what God has called us to do—our preaching must be bold and authoritative.

Preaching Must Be Text-Driven

The second mark of apostolic preaching is that it must be text-driven. The text itself is the real authority of the sermon and the preacher. Apostolic preaching is rooted in the Word of the living God. The sermon must be thoroughly biblical and entirely expository. In Peter's sermon there were five major citations of Old Testament Scripture that he weaved together. Note that Acts 2:17-21 is simply a reading of Joel 2:28-32. In Acts 2:25-28 we see Psalm 16:8-11. In Acts 2:30 he quoted Psalm 132:11. In Acts 2:31 Peter went back to Psalm 16:10. Finally, in Acts 2:34-35 Peter referenced Psalm 110:1. His entire message was rooted in the Scripture that he knew and had available to him. It is from this that I want us to observe five features of a text-driven sermon.

Read the Text

The first feature of a text-driven sermon is to read the text. Notice that Acts 2:16 begins, "This is what was spoken of through the prophet Joel." Expository preaching is not to begin by calling attention to what happened to you on the way to church. Rather, it is about calling attention to the Word of God. The preacher has nothing to say apart from the Word of God, for the preacher is a parrot of the Word. We are a cave that God has spoken into and our task is to echo His revelation.

Beginning a message with the reading of the Word is exactly what Ezra did in Nehemiah chapter 8: "Ezra the priest brought the law before the assembly of men…He read from it" (verses 2-3). It is what our Lord did in the synagogue in Nazareth: "The book of the prophet Isaiah was handed to Him. And He opened the book and found the place where it was written…" (Luke 4:17). It is what Paul told Timothy to do in 1 Timothy 4:13: "Give attention to the public reading of Scripture, to exhortation and teaching." Peter did what Ezra had done, what Christ had done, and what Paul had told every preacher to do.

Every preacher must begin with a reading of the Word of God because everything that will be said must originate from the text of Scripture. In Acts 2:16 Peter said, "This is what was spoken of through the prophet Joel." As Peter pointed out the occurrence of the pouring out of the Holy Spirit on the day of Pentecost, he used the Word of God to explain what had just happened and bring into focus the events with biblical support. Peter stood up, announced his text, and began, "'And it shall be in the last days,' God says…" (Acts 2:17). As a side note, notice the dual authorship of Scripture here. Verse 16 says Joel was the speaker, and verse 17 says God was the speaker. In the inspiration of Scripture, there is a primary Author and a secondary author. Joel was the secondary author; he was the instrument God used to record His message. Peter affirmed this in verse 17 when he clarified that it was God who was speaking what Joel had said. In other words, the real preacher on the day of Pentecost was not Joel or Peter, but God Himself.

God is speaking in this text, and the proof is in the personal pronouns that were used. For example, in verse 17 God said, "I will pour forth of My Spirit," and in verse 19 He said, "I will grant wonders in the sky above." The personal pronoun "I" refers to God; Joel and Peter are secondary to God, who is primary. In verse 18 we read, "Even on My bondslaves, both men and women, I will in those days pour forth of My Spirit." There, the personal pronoun "My" refers to God. So God is the real preacher here.

He is the one preaching on the day of Pentecost. Peter is simply a mouthpiece for what Joel has written, and Joel was inspired by God.

Explain the Text

After you read the text, you must explain the text. As we continue, we observe Peter explaining the Scriptures. He said, "It shall be that everyone who calls on the name of the Lord will be saved" (Acts 2:21). Then in verse 22 Peter explained the previous verse. We see an inseparable connection between the two verses. After challenging his audience to call on the name of the Lord, Peter provided the name they must call on for their eternal salvation. In verse 22 he stated the name of the Savior, Jesus the Nazarene. He then explained the ministry of this Savior: "A man attested to you by God with miracles and wonders and signs which God performed through Him in your midst, just as you yourselves know" (verse 22).

Peter finished his explanation of the Savior with the following words: "This Man, delivered over by the predetermined plan and foreknowledge of God, you nailed to a cross by the hands of godless men and put Him to death. But God raised him up again, putting an end to the agony of death, since it was impossible for Him to be held in its power" (verses 23-24). In Luke's account, these verses are merely an explanation of Joel 2:32. This is what expository preaching is—you read the text, then you explain the text. You explain it as it was meant to be interpreted, conveying the meaning of what the original author said, the historical setting in which it was said, and the grammatical sense of what was said.

Support the Text

After reading and explaining the text, the preacher is to support the text from other passages. Peter supported the central theme of his argument by tracing it throughout the Old Testament. He provided four strategic cross-references that bolstered his explanation of who the Savior is. The apostle was able to do this because the full counsel of God speaks with unity and clarity. Beginning in verse 25, Peter said, "David says of Him…," and with this statement he introduced a quote from Psalm 16:8-11:

> I have set the LORD continually before me; because He is at my right hand, I will not be shaken. Therefore my heart is glad and my glory rejoices; my flesh also will dwell securely. For You will not abandon my soul to Sheol; nor will You allow Your Holy One to undergo decay. You will make known to me the path of life; in Your presence is fullness of joy; in Your right hand there are pleasures forever.

Peter used Scripture to support Scripture and reinforce what he was saying. He defended the resurrection of the Lord Jesus Christ, which was mentioned in verse 24: "God raised Him up again." Then Peter said, "For David says of Him, 'I saw the Lord always in my presence'" (verse 25). Peter's intention is to alert his audience, as well as us, to the reality that David was not speaking of himself, but of a future and greater descendant of David who would come in the Messianic line, Jesus Christ Himself. In Psalm 16, David was looking beyond himself and beyond his own time to the coming of the Messiah.

Looking at Acts 2:25 in full, Peter said, "For David says of him, 'I saw the Lord always in my presence; for He is at my right hand, so that I will not be shaken.'" The passage speaks of Jesus' trust in God the Father as He approached the cross and hung upon it. Jesus knew the Father was with Him and would remain with Him until that time at high noon when God blocked out the sun and Jesus said "My God, My God, why have You forsaken Me?" (Matthew 27:46). For the first three hours upon the cross, Jesus knew that the Father was with Him. So in Acts 2:26 we read the Messiah proclaiming, "Therefore my heart was glad and my tongue exulted; moreover my flesh also will live in hope." The hope referred to here is the joy that was set before Jesus as He endured the cross (Hebrews 12:1-3). That is to say, Jesus knew that He would not die in vain, but that His death would secure the eternal salvation of all those for whom He was dying.

Peter's support of his assertion continues in verse 27, where he exposes an inter-Trinitarian conversation. Luke records what the Son is saying to the Father, "You will not abandon my soul to Hades, nor allow your Holy One to undergo decay. You have made known to me the ways of life; you will make me full of gladness with Your presence." Jesus knew that on the other side of death, His Father would raise Him from the grave. There would be a resurrection, and in that resurrection there would be fullness of joy and gladness in the presence of the Father.

The reason we know that Peter was speaking of Jesus and not David is because in verse 29 we read, "I may confidently say to you regarding the patriarch David that he both died and he was buried, and his tomb is with us to this day." Peter, with deep conviction, preached that David was not speaking of himself, for David is still in the grave. However, the grave of greater Son of David, the Lord Jesus Christ, is empty.

The second cross-reference Peter included in his sermon is Psalm 132:11: "God had sworn to him with an oath to seat one of his descendants on his throne" (Acts 2:30). Peter was undergirding what he had said in verse 24 regarding the resurrection of Jesus Christ. In verses 33-34 he continued, "Therefore having been exalted to the right hand of God, and having received from the Father the promise of the Holy Spirit, He has poured forth this which you both see and hear. For it was not David who ascended into heaven but he himself says…" Peter then quoted yet another text of Scripture, Psalm 110:1: "The Lord said to my Lord…" The first mention of "Lord" refers to God the Father, while "my Lord" refers to God the Son. The intent of this citation is to support what was said in Acts 2:21: "Everyone who calls on the name of the Lord will be saved." Peter is aiming to link the sermon very tightly with the salvation found in Christ—in the resurrection of Christ and the exaltation of Christ.

Synthesize the Text

The fourth feature of a text-driven sermon is the synthesis of the text. In Acts 2:36, Peter directs us to the conclusion of his message when he says, "Therefore let all the house of Israel know for certain that God has made Him both Lord and Christ—this Jesus whom you crucified." This expository sermon—this apostolic sermon—is not a compilation of disconnected theological thoughts with unrelated verses. In this message is a precise progression of logical and orderly thought. The Lord whom the people must call upon in verse 21 is the very Lord whom they have crucified in verse 23, the very Lord whom God has raised from the dead in verse 24, and the very Lord of whom God the Father has made both Lord and Christ in verse 36.

Apply the Text

The final feature of a text-driven sermon is application. Before Peter even had the opportunity to finish speaking, the people listening to him came to the startling realization, through the illuminating ministry of the Holy Spirit, that with their own hands they had put to death the Prince of Life: "Now when they heard this, they were pierced to the heart, and said to Peter and the rest of the apostles, 'Brethren, what shall we do?'" (verse 37). Peter had not even finished preaching, but the sermon was so arresting that the sinners were giving the invitation: "Brethren, what shall we do?" The people interrupted Peter's preaching because they were under the deep conviction of the Word of God. So in verse 38, Peter uses the second-person plural pronoun "you" and tells them, "Repent, and each of *you* be baptized in the name of Jesus Christ for the forgiveness of *your* sins; and *you* will receive the gift of the Holy Spirit" (emphases mine).

Like Peter's proclamation, our preaching must be personal and directional. We must give the application that spells out what the sinner and the saint must do. Expository preaching involves persuasion, appeal, invitation, begging, pleading, warning, and exhortation. Peter, in this sermon, exhorted the audience's will. He called for the verdict, and he pleaded for their decision.

It was said of Jonathan Edwards that his great preaching was used by God to spark the Great Awakening. This preaching included both doctrine and application, for the common Puritan sermon consisted of two main sections—doctrine, then application. It was said that in the doctrinal portion of his sermons Jonathan Edwards was merely bringing his cannons into place and packing in the gunpowder, and it was in the application portion that he fired them. I wonder how many times we fall short of firing our cannons as we set forth the doctrinal truths found in Scripture. Our sermons must include the imperative mood—they must incorporate the "you" that calls for a response. Text-driven preaching includes the application that God requires of His listeners.

Preaching Must Be Christ-Centered

The third mark of apostolic preaching, in addition to being authoritative and text-driven, is that it is Christ-centered. Peter's sermon was riveted on the person and work of Jesus Christ. In verse 22 we see the affirmation of Jesus as the Christ: "Men of Israel, listen to these words: Jesus the Nazarene, a man attested to you by God with miracles and wonders and signs which God performed through Him in your midst, just as you yourselves know…" Every miracle that Jesus performed was the finger of God from heaven pointing and saying, "This is My beloved son; hear Him."

Not only did Peter emphasize Jesus' qualification to be the Messiah, but he also taught about His foreordained death. Peter proclaimed that Jesus was "delivered over by the predetermined plan and foreknowledge of God" (Acts 2:23). Jesus Christ, the Lamb of God, was slain from before the foundation of the world. He was foreknown by the Father, and it was the Father's eternal decree that Jesus Christ would bear the sins of His people as He was nailed to the cross by the hands of godless men. Peter binds his audience's conscience and holds them directly accountable to God for the most heinous sin of all human history—the first-degree murder of the sinless Son of God. Peter then moves to the resurrection in verse 24: "But God raised him up again." In other words, Peter was saying to his listeners, "You thought you could put Him to death. You thought you would not have to deal with Him anymore. You thought you could wash your hands of the matter. You thought you could bury Him, and it would all be over. But God has raised Him from the dead."

Peter next moves to Jesus' exaltation. In verse 33 we read that Jesus was "exalted to the right hand of God." He was elevated to the place of highest honor, the place of absolute unrivaled sovereignty over heaven and hell. Thus, Jesus has the authority to send the Holy Spirit; He has the authority to convert His enemies; He has the authority to overcome circumstances; He has the authority to open eyes, ears, and hearts; He has the authority to grant repentance; He has the authority to bestow saving faith; and He has the authority to build His church. Peter declared the person and work of Jesus Christ on the day of Pentecost. This is what Paul was speaking of when he said we preach "Jesus Christ, and Him crucified" (1 Corinthians 2:2).

Peter did just that: "Therefore let all the house of Israel know for certain that God has made Him both Lord and Christ" (Acts 2:36).

Peter is not alone in church history with regard to preaching the centrality of Jesus Christ. Iain Murray, in his extraordinary book *The Forgotten Spurgeon*,[6] reveals that C.H. Spurgeon's ministry was focused entirely on preaching of the Lord Jesus Christ. Murray writes of an incident in which Spurgeon went into the Crystal Palace in London during the week in preparation of preaching there. One of the workers asked him, "Say something so we can test the acoustics." What came from Spurgeon's mouth was what was supreme in his heart—he said, "Behold the Lamb of the God who takes away the sin of the world." There was a worker up on the roof who heard the words and did not know Spurgeon was in the building. He thought he had heard the voice of God speaking to him. Startled, he went into the building, saw Spurgeon, and said to him, "I must be saved; I've heard the voice of God." Spurgeon responded, "What did He say?" The man answered, "Behold the Lamb of God who takes away the sin of the world."

There is another illustration of Spurgeon's fixation on the centrality of Jesus in preaching. In 1855 he preached a sermon entitled "Eternal Name." In the course of that sermon, Spurgeon depicted what would become of the world if the name of Jesus were to be removed from it. Unable to restrain his feelings, Spurgeon declared, "I would have no wish to be here without my Lord. And if the gospel be not true, I should bless God to annihilate me this instant, for I would not care to live if ye would destroy the name of Jesus Christ."[7]

> Apostolic preaching is an arrow that is fired
> like a laser to the target of the heart
> to magnify the glory of Jesus Christ.

Many years later, Mrs. Spurgeon reflected upon that night when her young husband preached that sermon. She reminisced about how her husband knew no greater joy than to preach the name of the Lord Jesus Christ.

She remembered that at the end of the sermon, after an entire hour of magnifying, elevating, and exalting the supreme Lordship of Jesus Christ, Spurgeon made a mighty effort to recover his voice, which had become hoarse. But all she could hear was him whispering, "Let my name perish but let Christ's name last forever. Jesus, crown Him Lord of all. You will not hear me say anything else."[8] Then Spurgeon fell backward into the chair that was behind the pulpit in exhaustion. It was Spurgeon's greatest glory to preach the name, the person, the work, and the terms of the Lord Jesus Christ. Apostolic preaching is an arrow that is fired like a laser to the target of the heart to magnify the glory of Jesus Christ.

Preaching Must Be Heart-Piercing

The fourth and final mark of apostolic preaching is that it must be heart-piercing. In Acts 2:37 Luke records the response of the audience to Peter's preaching and says, "When they heard this, they were pierced to the heart." In other words, Luke is saying the audience felt as if they had been stabbed with a knife. This is the only kind of preaching that brings about such a soul-rending result.

Dramatic plays and video clips are not going to produce this type of response. Nor a man-centered sermon series on how to have a happy vacation. Only bold and authoritative preaching that is text-driven and Christ-centered can bring about this effect in the hearts of sinners. When Peter's listeners "were pierced to the heart," they cried out, "Brethren, what shall we do?" (Acts 2:37). And Peter answered by preaching repentance to them. He told the people to acknowledge and turn from their sin, renounce self and self-righteousness, and throw themselves upon the mercy of the Lord Jesus Christ. Earlier in the sermon he had promised, "Everyone who calls on the name of the Lord will be saved" (verse 21), and he repeated this at the end: "The promise is for you and your children and for all who are far off, as many as the Lord our God will call to Himself" (Acts 2:39).

Peter relied upon the sovereign election of God to call out those sinners who were elect before the foundation of the world. He believed in the sufficiency of God's Word and the sufficiency of the Holy Spirit to uphold the text and uphold Christ so that God would be pleased to call sinners to Himself.

The Preaching God Honors

We must ask the question, Did God honor this preaching? The answer is in Acts 2:41: "So then, those who had received his word were baptized; and that day there were added about three thousand souls." God is pleased to honor the preaching of His Word that lifts up the name of the Son of God. Richard Baxter said, "I preached as never sure to preach again; and as a dying man to dying men."[9] Every time you step up to the pulpit, may you preach as though it is the final sermon you will ever proclaim.

This is the passion and the power of apostolic preaching. Such preaching is bold, text-driven, Christ-centered, and heart-piercing. May God raise up expositors who will herald the Word far and wide.

PRAYER

Father, thank You for the glories and the majesty of Christ. Thank You for our Savior and Your predetermined plan that commissioned Him into this world. Thank You that at the fullness of time He was born under the law to perfectly keep every demand and every requirement of the law. Thank You for His determination to set His face like a flint toward Jerusalem and to be lifted up from the earth upon that cross for us.

Thank You, Father for taking our sins and transferring them to Christ that He might make them His very own. We thank You that He bore our sin, absorbed Your wrath, and was raised in glory. As You send us into the world to proclaim the great message of salvation, may we preach as Peter preached on the day of Pentecost. May there be passion and urgency as we lift high that name that shall endure forever, the name of our Lord Jesus Christ. In His name we pray, Amen.

PREACHING IN THE SPIRIT'S POWER

"I determined to know nothing among you
except Jesus Christ, and Him crucified."

1 CORINTHIANS 2:2

8

PREACHING IN THE SPIRIT'S POWER

Tom Pennington
Shepherds' Conference 2010

1 Corinthians 2:1-5

W̶e are painfully aware of our inadequacy as preachers. Many Sundays in the moments before I enter the pulpit, I find myself repeating the words Martin Luther often prayed before he preached: "Dear Lord God, I want to preach so that you are glorified...Although I probably cannot make it turn out well, won't you make it turn out well?"[1] More often my prayer comes from the words of Paul in 1 Corinthians 2:5—"Father, help me to preach in demonstration of the Spirit and of power." That must be the goal and the prayer of every true preacher of the Word of God. Those remarkable words are the heart of the clearest statement of Paul's philosophy of preaching found anywhere in his letters.

The apostle Paul visited the Greek city of Corinth on his second missionary journey in AD 51. According to Acts 18, he stayed there for 18 months. Three years after Paul had departed from Corinth, while he was in Ephesus, he heard some troubling news. A prominent member of the church, Chloe, wrote to Paul or perhaps even travelled across the Aegean Sea to bring the report that serious divisions had erupted in the church at Corinth.

Enamored with the Method

Paul began his letter to the Corinthians by addressing that serious problem. He wrote, "Now I mean this, that each one of you is saying, 'I am of Paul,' and 'I am of Apollos,' and 'I am of Cephas,' and 'I of Christ'" (1 Corinthians 1:12). Why this division? In verse 17, Paul elaborated on the issue that was dividing the church, which had to do with "cleverness of speech." The problem in Corinth was not primarily about doctrine, but style. It was not about what was preached, but how it was preached. Ultimately, what divided the church in Corinth was something that the people had embraced from the culture around them—they were enamored by eloquent rhetoric.

Scholars who have researched the situation in first-century Corinth say that Corinth was home to a very popular school of Greek rhetoric promoted by a group called the Sophists.[2] The Sophists were itinerant intellectuals who taught rhetoric for a fee. They traveled from city to city trying to amaze people with their speaking in order to attract paying students.

Philosophically, the Sophists were relativists. That is, they were not convinced about the certainty of truth. For the Sophists, then, communication was more about style than substance, which set this school of rhetoric against even the great philosophers Aristotle and Plato.

The Sophists were also pragmatists. They contextualized their message to get the results they wanted. They were primarily after personal advancement, applause, status, and the wealth that came with these things. They intentionally chose content and the form of that content which would most please the crowd. Their intent was to build their own personal prestige and their greatest concern was results, not truth.

Duane Litfin, in his book *St. Paul's Theology of Proclamation*, describes their priority this way: "The orator began by determining what results he wanted to achieve and then he shaped his message accordingly. The message was the manipulated variable...and it was up to the orator by the sheer power of his rhetorical gifts, his training, his experience, to create a message that would produce those results."[3] This group in Corinth was selling what one writer called "an applause-generating, consumer-oriented rhetoric."[4]

Nothing was more important in Greek culture than the ability to speak in a way that persuaded others. If you could speak with some measure of eloquence, then you were considered to be intelligent, cultured, and high-class. In fact, the English word *sophisticated* comes from the Greek word *sophos,* which means "skilled" or "wise." Tragically, the believers in Corinth played right into the hands of these teachers and were attracted to those who spoke eloquently. First Corinthians 1 says there were some believers who rallied around Apollos—their slogan was, "We're of Apollos." There were others who were impressed by Paul's ability to speak. Their slogan was, "We are of Paul." Still others claimed Peter or Christ as their favored orator.

Paul, however, explained to the Corinthians that they were wrong in being enamored with any one person's speaking style. In 1 Corinthians 1, he said God intentionally wanted to save sinners in a way that would demolish any reason for human pride and wisdom. To accomplish this task, God chose a foolish message—the gospel. He chose a foolish method— preaching. And He chose foolish people to redeem—a bunch of nobodies.

All through 1 Corinthians chapter 1, Paul made it clear that in matters related to the gospel and salvation, God's ultimate goal was to remove any reason for human pride and to bring all glory to Himself. That's the message through the end of chapter 1. Paul then said that when he came to preach to the Corinthians, he had done so in a way that complemented God's goal. Christ had not sent Paul to preach the gospel in cleverness of speech, for Paul's success in Corinth had nothing to do with him, his ingenuity, or his technique. Paul's preaching and the response it generated was entirely a work of the Spirit.

In 1 Corinthians 2:1-5, Paul contrasted his approach to preaching with the techniques the Sophists used in their rhetoric:

> When I came to you, brethren, I did not come with superiority of speech or of wisdom, proclaiming to you the testimony of God. For I determined to know nothing among you except Jesus Christ, and Him crucified. I was with you in weakness and in fear and in much trembling, and my message and my preaching were not in persuasive words of wisdom, but in demonstration of the Spirit and of power, so that your faith would not rest on the wisdom of men, but on the power of God.

Paul's message in these verses is clear and direct: Preaching that exalts God must always be "in demonstration of the Spirit and of power." The question is, how do we preach like that? In this text we discover the personal commitments Paul made in his own preaching—commitments that enabled him to rely completely on the Spirit's power and not his own. He was not dependent on his personality, the power of his own gifts, or some human technique.

> If we are going to preach in demonstration
> of the Spirit and of power, we must focus on
> the message and not our own glory.

Keys to Preaching in the Spirit's Power

So what are the crucial commitments we need to make to preach in a way that demonstrates the Spirit's presence and power?

Focus on God's Message and Not Personal Glory

The first commitment we must make is to focus on God's message and not personal glory. Paul wrote in 1 Corinthians 2:1, "When I came to you, brethren, I did not come with superiority of speech or of wisdom, proclaiming to you the testimony of God." The Greek word translated "superiority" literally means "a projection or something that rises above what is around it." The verb form of the word means "to stand out, to rise above, to outdo, to excel." Paul did not come to Corinth attempting to make his speech or wisdom stand out from that of other orators. His aspiration wasn't to outdo anyone, nor did he preach in an attempt to distinguish himself. Paul's philosophy of preaching was this: "We do not preach ourselves but Christ Jesus as Lord, and ourselves as your bond-servants for Jesus' sake" (2 Corinthians 4:5).

If we are going to preach in demonstration of the Spirit and of power, we must focus on the message and not our own glory. The Scottish pastor

James Denney understood this philosophy of preaching. To help him remember, he had these words framed and hung in his church: "No man can bear witness to Christ and to himself at the same time. No man can give the impression that he himself is clever, and that Christ is mighty to save."[5] Similarly, Paul refused to promote his own cleverness. In his *speech*—that is, his style of speaking. Or in his *wisdom*—that is, his content.

As Paul made his point, he used the very terms the orators in Corinth loved. He said, "I didn't come to exalt myself, to excel in some way, to distinguish myself. Instead, my focus was on God and His message. I came proclaiming to you the testimony of God." The Greek word translated "proclaiming" was used often in the first century to speak of an official or authoritative announcement. We are not called to "share" the Word and we certainly aren't called to be "part of a conversation" about the Word. We are called to *proclaim* the Word, and to do so with authority.

Announcing Christ

What are we to announce? First Corinthians 2:1 says, "The testimony of God." Like Paul, we are to declare with authority God's own testimony—especially the testimony about His Son. Paul elaborated on this in verse 2: "I determined to know nothing among you except Jesus Christ, and Him crucified." Some people think that in this passage, Paul was announcing a change in his preaching style. They say that when the apostle went to Athens, his message was more philosophical. But then after his "failure" on Mars Hill, he realized he should change his approach.

But there's no evidence in Acts 17 that Paul was disappointed with his ministry in Athens. Preaching Christ and Him crucified was Paul's message from day one, when he met the risen Savior on the Damascus Road. Notice what Paul wrote in his very first New Testament letter, the book of Galatians. He described the Galatians as those "before whose eyes Jesus Christ was publicly portrayed as crucified" (3:1). Paul, from the beginning of his ministry, preached Jesus Christ and Him crucified. This was always his approach, and he never deviated from it.

What does it mean to preach Christ and Him crucified? It doesn't mean that all Paul taught about was Jesus and the cross. For example, in Acts 18:11, we learn that Paul settled in Corinth for a year and half and taught all of the Old Testament scriptures to the Christians there. Surely his ministry in Corinth was similar to what he had done in Ephesus. Remember what he said to the Ephesian elders in Acts 20:27? "I did not shrink from declaring to you the whole counsel of God."

To preach Christ and Him crucified does not mean to declare the simple gospel message and nothing else. If we do that, we are missing out on the purpose of corporate worship, and we will also starve the sheep. Instead, Paul was saying that everything we preach must ultimately be rooted in and founded upon the truth that Jesus is the Messiah. Paul's preaching found its center in Jesus Christ and Him crucified.

Staying Focused

Twenty years ago, I was diagnosed with the eye disease glaucoma. Once or twice a year I take a visual field test that checks my peripheral vision to make sure I have no additional optic nerve damage. During the test, the technician props my head onto a device that holds my chin still, and tells me to keep my eyes focused on a red pinpoint of light directly in front of me. As I stare at that red light, one at a time little pinpoints of white light begin to show up in my peripheral field of vision. When I see a white light, I'm supposed to push a button. I dislike this test because it's very intense, and after several seconds of staring at that red light and not seeing any pinpoints of light in my peripheral vision, I wonder if maybe I missed one, so I'm tempted to push the button just in case.

What's interesting about this test is that if your eyes wander from the red light for even a second, a buzzer sounds to tell you that you've lost your focus. You have to stay focused on the center so that any other lights you see are visible only in your peripheral vision. That illustrates what Paul meant when he said, "We must keep our preaching centered on Christ." Whatever our subject may be or whatever passage we are preaching from, we must keep our eyes centered on Christ and His cross. I don't mean we ought to distort a text by spiritualizing it to include Christ. However, the great theme of the Bible is that God is redeeming a people by His Son, for His Son, to His own glory. Whatever your passage, it's somehow developing that theme. Our responsibility, then, as ministers of the New

Covenant, is to show our listeners how that theme is interwoven in the text we preach.

Charles Spurgeon loved to tell his students the story of a young preacher who gave a sermon while an older and more experienced preacher sat in the audience. Afterward, the young preacher asked the older man, "What did you think of my message?"

The older pastor replied, "It was a very poor sermon, indeed."

The young man said, "I don't understand. I studied a long time. I pored over the text. Was my explanation wrong? Were my arguments weak? Were my illustrations inappropriate?"

The older pastor said, "No, all those things were fine. But it was still a poor sermon."

Exasperated, the young preacher said, "Tell me why."

The older preacher answered, "Because there was no Christ in it."

The young man responded, "Christ wasn't in the text. You have to preach the text."

"Don't you know," said the older man, "that from every town and every village in England there is a road to London? So also from every text in Scripture there is a road to Christ. Your business, when you get to a text, is to say, 'What is the road to Christ?' and then make sure your sermon follows that road."[6]

Every sermon we preach must ultimately point to Christ and Him crucified. That means our sermons need to include not only the historical facts of the crucifixion and resurrection, but also the meaning of Jesus' death and resurrection, and the nature of the atonement. Throughout his letters, Paul explained Jesus' death and used profoundly rich theological terms to do so—terms that today are foreign to many professing Christians. For example, there's *substitution*—Jesus, the innocent one, died in the place of the guilty. There's *imputation*—God credits to the sinner the righteousness of Christ, and He credits to Christ the sin of the one who believes.

There's also *propitiation*—during those six hours on the cross, Christ satisfied the infinite wrath of God against the sin of everyone who will ever believe. Then there's *justification*—we are declared right before God, the Judge, on the basis of the righteousness of Jesus Christ that we receive by faith.

Paul taught both the historicity of the cross and the theological implications of it. He wasn't concerned that someone might think his teaching was the moral equivalent of divine child abuse, as some people claim. The heart of Paul's ministry of the Word was Jesus Christ *and* the facts, nature, and ramifications of His death.

Paul didn't try to contextualize the gospel message to make it more palatable to people. In fact, in Corinth, Paul dwelt on the very element of the Christian message that was most in conflict with the surrounding culture. The Corinthians thought the message was foolish, and yet that's the message Paul preached.

The sad truth is that a portion of today's evangelical church has allowed its focus to drift. Some pastors and churches have taken their eyes off the pinpoint of light at the center and let their focus wander to things that should only be in the periphery. Paul wanted us to understand that ultimately, our preaching must focus on the person of Jesus Christ and the doctrine of the atonement. What that means, in practical terms, is that we must not choose our next sermon series based on what we think will draw the largest crowd. For example, Paul didn't focus on how to have better relationships or how to communicate better. We are called to preach the Scriptures, and when we do, we are to do so without letting our eyes wander from the focal point, which is Jesus Christ and His death and atonement.

Having Christ and Him crucified at the center of our preaching will also determine the boundaries of our fellowship. The truth of the gospel ought to be more important to us than becoming cobelligerents, even on important issues like abortion, the sanctity of marriage, or social justice. We should be more concerned about protecting the gospel than the planet. We should be more passionate about defending the atonement than the environment. We cannot allow any cause to become more important to us than Christ—not our personal glory, not some pet doctrine or program, not church growth, not a social agenda, and not some façade of Christian unity.

D.A. Carson was right when he said, "Whenever the periphery is in danger of displacing the center, we are not far removed from idolatry."[7] If we want our preaching to put the power of God's Spirit on display, then we first have to make the same commitment that Paul made: to focus on God's message and not on personal glory.

Depend on God's Grace and Not Personal Ability

There's a second commitment Paul made that we also need to make: We must depend on God's grace and not personal ability. In 1 Corinthians 2:3 Paul transitioned from the content of his preaching to the content of his heart. He said, "I was with you in weakness and in fear and in much trembling."

There are two primary ways to understand this verse. Paul may have been referring to his physical circumstances. It's possible that he was physically weak when he arrived in Corinth, perhaps because he was ill. Or it's possible that Paul was afraid for his own safety when he came to Corinth (see Acts 18). But based on the context, it's best to see Paul again contrasting himself and his attitude with the Sophists. Paul was not referring to his physical weakness, but to his own attitude about preaching: "I was with you in weakness and in fear and in much trembling." In Ephesians 6:5, Paul used two of these words, "fear and trembling," when he told slaves to obey their earthly masters. Paul was describing a kind of conscientious anxiety. That's the attitude necessary for properly declaring the Word of God.

Personal danger did not make Paul tremble. It was the weight of responsibility that he shouldered in his preaching ministry. As Bible commentator Gordon Fee said, "Paul seems overwhelmed by the task before him."[8] When Paul preached, he was painfully aware of his own weakness. He had a deep sense of his inadequacy for doing what the Lord had called him to do. It was with fear and trembling that Paul came into the pulpit.

It's important to remember that when Paul came to Corinth, he had already been preaching the gospel for some 20 years. Yet he still had an attitude of humility. What's notable is that Paul's attitude was exactly the opposite of the attitude exuded by the speakers whom the Corinthians so greatly admired. One of the distinguishing traits of the Sophists was their supreme self-confidence when they got up to speak. In that culture, self-assurance was considered an essential for an effective orator. One ancient writer described the attitude of one Sophist this way: "He appeared before his audience as one who was entering to win glory for himself, and was confident that he could not fail."[9]

Paul, however, felt inadequate for the task of proclaiming the testimony of God. He stated this frequently. In 1 Corinthians 15:10 he said, "By the grace of God I am what I am, and His grace toward me did not prove vain; but I labored even more than all of them"—that is, more than all the apostles—"yet not I, but the grace of God with me." The reason Paul was able to labor so effectively had nothing to do with him. Rather, it was the grace of God in him.

Paul reaffirmed this in 2 Corinthians 2:14, where he revealed that he had been given the responsibility to manifest "the sweet aroma of the knowledge of [Christ] in every place." In verse 16 we see that in some cases that sweet aroma brings death, and in other cases it brings life. Paul added, "Who is adequate for these things? For we are not like many, peddling the Word of God, but as from sincerity, but as from God, we speak in Christ in the sight of God" (verses 16-17). We see this again in 2 Corinthians 3:4-6: "Such confidence we have through Christ toward God. Not that we are adequate in ourselves to consider anything as coming from ourselves, but our adequacy is from God, who also made us adequate." Like Paul, we are utterly inadequate to do what God has called us to do. Our only hope is in His grace.

Martin Luther understood the inadequacy of the preacher. In May 1532, Luther was trying to encourage his friend Anthony Lauterbach, who had been called as pastor of the Castle Church in Wittenberg. Luther looked back at his own experience at the beginning of his ministry and explained "how I feared the pulpit." He continued, "I advanced more than 15 arguments to Dr. Staupitz, and with them I declined my call, but they did me no good. When I finally said, 'Dr. Staupitz, you are taking my life. I shall not live a quarter year if you make me preach.' He replied, 'God needs wise people in heaven, too.'"[10] Luther understood his inadequacy and his inability.

Paul came to the pulpit with that same sense of fear and humility. Is this our attitude when we preach? If we're honest with ourselves, I think we are all tempted to believe that we can preach God's Word in our own ability—that we have the capacity and the tools to understand the Bible in all its depth and richness. We can even convince ourselves that somehow, by our own skill, we can take that Word and make people understand it, respond to it, and be changed by it. Whenever such thoughts cross our mind, we need to repent in sackcloth and ashes.

John Calvin wrote, "Those who intrude themselves confidently, or who discharge the ministry of the Word with an easy mind, as though they were fully equal to the task, are ignorant both of themselves and of the task."[11] Self-confidence is deadly in a preacher of the gospel. We see this in the story of the preacher who entered the pulpit with great confidence. When he was done, it was clear to everyone that the sermon was a terrible disappointment. He came out of the pulpit greatly humbled, and later, an elder of the church gave him this wise advice: "If you had entered the pulpit the way you left it, you would have left the pulpit the way you entered it."

Our confidence cannot be in ourselves—in our personality, our ability to communicate, in our skills with the original languages, our intellect, our experiences, or our education. We must depend on God's grace to preach in a way that demonstrates the Spirit's power.

Like Paul, we need to cultivate an awareness of our own weakness and inadequacy. We must surrender every shred of self-confidence and approach the Word of God with fear and trembling. When we are weak, God manifests His power; and only then does He get all the glory. As 2 Corinthians 4:7 says, "We have this treasure in earthen vessels, so that the surpassing greatness of the power will be of God and not from ourselves." To preach in the demonstration of the Spirit and of power, we must focus on God's message and not personal glory. We must depend on God's grace and not personal ability.

Trust in the Spirit's Power and Not Any Human Method or Technique

The third commitment a preacher must make is to trust in the Spirit's power and not in any human method or technique. Note what Paul said: "My message and my preaching were not in persuasive words of wisdom, but in demonstration of the Spirit and of power" (1 Corinthians 2:4). Paul made sure that the power of his persuasion didn't rest in him, his form, or his delivery. When he said "my message," he was referring to the content of his preaching. And "my preaching" refers to the style with which he presented his message. Paul intended these two words as a kind of hendiadys—that is, two words that combine into one idea, like "sick and tired."

Paul was saying that nothing about his preaching—content, form, or delivery style—was done with persuasive words of human wisdom. If you had been sitting in first-century Corinth, hearing these words from Paul would have shocked you. As we saw earlier, the Sophists' primary goal was to use their wisdom and delivery to persuade people—and the people of Corinth were enamored by this. By contrast, Paul wrote, "My message and my preaching were not in persuasive words of wisdom, but in demonstration of the Spirit and of power." The Greek word translated "demonstration" is a word that the Sophists loved. It occurs only here in the New Testament, but in Greek rhetoric it was a technical term used to speak of compelling evidence or proof.

Here's what Paul wants us to understand: The compelling factor in preaching is not our personal powers of persuasion. It is not the brilliance of our arguments. It does not lie in the structure of our message. It doesn't rest in the manner of our delivery. The compelling demonstration in our preaching must always be the Spirit and His power working through the message.

Very few of us today are tempted to use the techniques of first-century Greek rhetoric in an attempt to persuade an audience. But we're still faced with the temptation to rely on human methods and techniques of persuasion rather than depend on the power of the Spirit.

We need to search our hearts and honestly ask ourselves, "What human methods or techniques are we tempted to rely on? What do we believe really persuades people when we preach?" Maybe our confidence is in the style of our delivery. Perhaps we figure that if we expend a lot of energy, pump up the volume, sweat through a couple of handkerchiefs, use catchy sayings, and close the service with an emotional story, we'll persuade people. Then there are those who believe the best approach is to speak with a quiet and intense sincerity. The goal is to make the sermon sound like a conversation. While our style of communication ought to be a natural expression of who we are, we cannot think for a moment that's where the power lies when it comes to preaching.

Still others are tempted to put their confidence in the visual arts, drama, the right lighting, or some other visual or experiential approach. There's a big emphasis on setting the right atmosphere.

If our confidence for persuading people is in anything but the power of the Spirit, we will never know His power in our preaching.

Even those who are committed to biblical exposition can end up relying on some human technique or method. Expositors can be tempted to put their confidence in long hours of study, careful exegesis, syntactical analysis, homiletical skills, parallel outline points, and passionate delivery. As Martyn Lloyd-Jones has said, "We can easily become pulpiteers rather than preachers."[12]

Henry Ward Beecher had a name for sermons designed to put our preaching skills on display—he called them "Nebuchadnezzar sermons; is this not Babylon the great, that I have built myself, by the might of my power and for the glory of my majesty?" Beecher went on to say, "Would to God that these preachers would go, like Nebuchadnezzar, to grass for a time. If like him, they would return sane and humble."[13]

While it's true that careful exegesis and diligent sermon preparation are essential, still, if our confidence for persuading people is in anything but the power of the Spirit, we will never know His power in our preaching, for He will not share His glory with us.

Preaching in the Spirit's Power—Proclaiming God's Word

What exactly is preaching in the demonstration of the Spirit and of power? Some respected men in the history of the church have thought of preaching in the Spirit's power as some kind of a special experience—they speak of a special anointing to preach. It's true that the New Testament uses two different Greek word groups to speak of two kinds of Spirit-filling. One of them speaks of a condition of the soul. According to Ephesians 5:18, we are to allow the Spirit to fill us with the Word of God (cf. Colossians 3:16). The other describes a filling with the Spirit that is a special empowering, a divine enablement to fulfill a specific task at a designated time. And some ministers interpret 1 Corinthians 2:4 as saying, "I ought to seek a special empowerment to preach."

However, the context of 1 Corinthians 2:4 makes it clear that's not what Paul had in mind. Here Paul directly linked preaching in the demonstration of the Spirit's power to the Word of God. In the rest of 1 Corinthians 2, he emphasizes that the Spirit revealed the Word of God, inspired the Word of God, and illumines our understanding of the Word of God. Paul's point was that the Spirit's power is demonstrated *through* the Word. He said this to the church in Thessalonica as well: "Our gospel did not come to you in word only, but also in power and in the Holy Spirit" (1 Thessalonians 1:5). In other words, the Holy Spirit was manifesting His power through the words of the gospel that Paul preached.

How can you and I preach in demonstration of the Spirit and His power? Not by seeking some mystical experience, but *by preaching the truth the Spirit inspired, and doing so in complete dependence upon Him.* As a result, the Spirit will take that Word preached and He will do what you and I could never do. He will illumine, He will give life, and He will change minds and hearts. When Paul speaks of preaching in demonstration of the Spirit and of power, he is not referring to power that resides in the preacher, a powerful experience that happens to him, or some powerful technique he employs. Rather, Paul means the power that is in God's Word when it is accurately preached and energized by the Spirit.

In the first two chapters of 1 Corinthians, we learn that God has a great eternal plan for redeeming sinners. He decided on this plan so that no human being would be able to boast before Him. God chose a message that undermines all human wisdom. And He chose for preaching to be the method by which this message would spread—a method that cuts across human wisdom in every age. Why? So that He alone would get the glory.

When you and I change the emphasis of the message away from Christ and Him crucified or the means of delivering that message, terrible things happen. The cross of Christ is made void (1 Corinthians 1:17)—that is, we empty the message of the cross of its power. When we change the method or the message, we also rob God of His glory (1 Corinthians 1:30-31). In 1 Corinthians 2:5 Paul adds yet another terrible outcome of tampering with the message and the method. He declared that the reason he did not preach persuasive words of human wisdom was "so that your faith would not rest on the wisdom of men, but on the power of God." When we elevate ourselves rather than God's message, when we depend on our own abilities rather than God's grace, and when we trust in human methods or techniques rather than the Spirit's power, then we cause people's faith to rest on human wisdom and not God's power.

Gordon Fee, commenting on this passage, challenges us all: "Paul's point needs a fresh hearing. What he is rejecting is not preaching, not even persuasive preaching; rather, it is the real danger in all preaching, self-reliance."[14] The danger lies in forgetting that lives are changed when the gospel is proclaimed through human weakness and accompanied by the powerful work of the Spirit.

We live in a culture that is almost identical to that which existed in Corinth. We are faced with the very same dilemma that confronted Paul when he first arrived in that city. May God help us to follow the preaching philosophy of the apostle Paul, who preached in the power of the Spirit by (1) focusing on God's message and His Son instead of personal glory, (2) depending on God's grace and not our personal ability, and (3) trusting in the Spirit's power and not any human method or technique. When we approach preaching with these commitments, then it will be in demonstration of the Spirit and of power.

PRAYER

Father, forgive us for the times when we handle Your Word with a sense of self-confidence and we trust in something other than Your Word and Your Spirit. We repent and we ask that You would give us, through this passage, a fresh reminder of how we are to approach the task of preaching.

Lord, none of us are comparable to the apostle Paul, and yet he realized the inadequacies in his own life. May we embrace our weaknesses and frailty, and may we realize that when we acknowledge our insufficiency we are opening ourselves for the work of the Spirit. Father, use us to build Your church—to see people come to faith in Christ and see believers grow and be edified. We pray that You would do this in demonstration of the Spirit and His power. Amen.

The Art of Crafting a Life–Changing Sermon

"Woe is me if I do not preach the gospel."

1 Corinthians 9:16

9

The Art of Crafting a Life-Changing Sermon

Rick Holland
Shepherds' Conference 2010

Selected Scriptures

In order to refine my preaching, I've tried to place myself into situations where I'm stretched as a preacher. For example, earlier in my ministry, I served in a couple of youth pastoral positions that allowed me the opportunity to preach on a weekly basis to students. This experience was invaluable—if you really want to learn how to preach, then you should preach to junior high, high school, and college students. They don't have the courtesy to pretend that you're interesting when you're not. Likewise, preaching to young people helped me to figure out the dynamic of bringing the exegetical and delivery aspects of a sermon together in an environment where gaining people's interest is very difficult and clarity demands simplicity.

I've also had the privilege of studying at The Master's Seminary and Southern Baptist Theological Seminary. At both schools, I learned under the example of excellent preachers who have served as role models for my own pulpit practices.

Even with these helpful experiences, I still find myself learning how to preach more effectively. There's always room for us as preachers to develop better outlines, propositions, introductions, transitions, illustrations, applications, implications, and conclusions. There is no end to the work of mastering the art of delivering a good sermon.

There are some Sundays when, after giving a sermon, I feel like writing a letter of resignation. If you haven't felt that level of discouragement before, then you haven't preached long enough. I can usually tell how I did on a Sunday based on how my wife reacts during the drive home. If she says something to me about the sermon in the parking lot, I did okay. If we pass a certain landmark before she says anything, then it was "iffy." If we get to the highway before she speaks, there were problems in the sermon that she wants to talk about. And if we make it all the way home without her saying anything, then that usually indicates something bad.

Yet I still come back to the pulpit week in and week out because there's nothing else I would rather do than preach the Word of God. I aspire to excel still more in preaching, and my goal is to help you do the same.

Preaching and the Current Culture

As if our own idiosyncrasies weren't enough of a barrier to preaching well, we also live in a culture that does not hold expository preaching in high regard. This is nothing new. For example, in 1928, Harry Emerson Fosdick published an essay in *Harper's Magazine* that was entitled, "What's Wrong with Preaching?" He was one of the most prominent liberal ministers of his day, and he called for a type of preaching that was more relevant and involved more congregational experiences. Here's what he wrote:

> Many preachers indulge habitually in what they call expository sermons. They take a passage from the Scripture, and proceeding on the assumption that the people attending church that morning are deeply concerned about what the passage means, they spend their half hour or more on historical exposition of the verse or chapter, ending with some upended practical application to the auditors. Could any procedure be more surely predestined to dullness and futility? Who seriously supposes that, as a matter of fact, one in a hundred of the congregation cares to start with about what Moses, Isaiah, Paul, or John meant in those special verses, or came to church deeply concerned about it. Nobody else who talks to the public so

assumes that the vital interests of the people are located in the meaning of words spoken 2,000 years ago.[1]

Almost a century later, this sentiment is still prevalent in many churches today. There are pastors who, like Fosdick, disdain expository preaching. At the same time, Fosdick gives voice to what many people today are asking: "How is it that the things that happened in the Bible have any relevance, bearing, or meaning to my life today?"

This surfaces a divide that exists between the scholar and the listener. Scholars are mostly concerned with what the text of Scripture meant. They focus on what happened back in Corinth, in Rome, or in Hosea's time. Those who sit in the congregation, on the other hand, are mainly interested in what the text means to them in their own world. Broadly, scholars care about what the text *meant*; those who listen in the pew care about what it *means*. And it's the pastor who stands in between those two worlds and brings them together in a sermon. He does so by explaining what the text meant and showing its relevance for today. And he should be controlled by this mammoth principle—the text can never *mean* something today that it did not *meant* originally.

The preacher's job is to move from the past to the present, from the historical to the contemporary, from the particular to the universal. He has the difficult task of moving from the specifics in the Word to the principles that can be preached. Our homiletics must come from our hermeneutics. In fact, preaching is public hermeneutics. Every time a preacher opens the Bible and tells his people what it says and means, he is teaching them, by example, how they are to approach Scripture in their devotional time and personal Bible study. He is providing a pattern for how people are to understand and apply God's Word.

When you preach, your people...need to understand the original context of the text before they can apply what it means for them today.

If I have one criticism of preaching today, it is that it starts with the contemporary and tries to go backward, instead of beginning with the past and moving forward. Historian George Marsden wrote this about the critics of the Great Awakening, who did not see the value in preaching the historical context of a biblical passage:

> In the midst of the Great Awakening, Edwards made a revealing comment about the effects of preaching. During intense periods of awakenings, evangelists often preach to the same audience daily or even more frequently, multiple times a day. Opponents of the awakening argued that people could not possibly remember what they heard in all these sermons. [2]

Jonathan Edwards responded to these critics with the statement: "The main benefit that is obtained by preaching is by the impression made upon the mind in the time of it, and not by the effect that arises afterwards by a remembrance of what was delivered." [3] Edwards was right—preaching is designed to shock people with the living reality of God, and to take them from their contemporary world back into the Bible. When you preach, your people need to go back, put on sandals, and "experience the humidity" of that day. They need to understand the original context of the text before they can apply what it means for them today.

As preachers, it's so easy for us to come to a text, find a little lesson, get up, talk about it, illustrate it, apply it, cry, laugh, tell a joke, leave, get a pat on the back, and think we've done a great job. In contrast, I want to talk about life-changing preaching that builds a bridge from exegesis to an artfully crafted sermon that truly affects people. We're going to look at ten principles of life-changing preaching, each beginning with the letter *I*.

Principles of Life-Changing Preaching

Indisputable Preaching

Preaching God's Word God's Way, for God's People

The first *I* of life-changing preaching is *indisputable preaching*. Indisputability comes from preaching God's Word, God's way, to God's people, for God's glory. It's being accurate, clear, and making sure to present the meaning of the biblical text rather than human opinions. Indisputable preaching can only come from discerning and explaining the authorial intent of the biblical author. The crown jewel of all exposition—the result of all exegesis—is being able to answer the question, "What did this text originally mean to those to whom it was originally written?"

The only way our preaching will be indisputable is if we get to this crown jewel. If our content is what the Bible says, all that the Bible says, and no more than what the Bible says, we are speaking an audible articulation of God's voice. As preachers, our mandate is to preach the truth—the Word. Therefore, if someone has an argument with what we say, it ought to be an argument with what the Book says.

I've had firsthand experience with an extremely conservative church that lacked indisputability. As a recently converted high school student, I was excited about the Lord and had an older man disciple me. One day when he took me out to lunch he reprimanded me for about an hour because some of my hair was touching the top of my ear. The conversation grieved my conscience and I was so overwhelmed that I got a haircut the next day. As I continued attending the church, I was given plenty of other "corrections" that had no umbilical cord attached the Bible. I could dispute much of what was said because the church attempted to say more than what the text said.

Our job as pastors is to rely only on the text that's in front of us and mine the original meaning from it. We must understand what Moses meant, what Haggai meant, and what Paul meant in the original context to the original readers. By contrast, there are some who say, "Well, you can't possibly know that; the Bible is so old." This attitude leads to a reader-response methodology in which the meaning of a passage is ultimately based on what the reader wants it to mean. The objective truth then becomes completely subjective. Sadly, that kind of thinking has made its way into the pulpit, where many pastors are now attempting to create an experience that lets people interpret God's Word any way they want to. These preachers say the Bible is all about "what it means to you."

But that wasn't God's intention when He wrote the Bible. He wants the reader to understand the authorial intent. There's a test I apply to myself whenever I prepare a sermon. For example, while I was preaching through Proverbs, whenever I made my final pass through my notes I asked the question, "What would Solomon say if he heard this sermon? Would he agree with me, or would he stand up and say, 'I'm sorry, but that's not what I meant when I said that.'"

When you preach, do you explain to your people what the author meant? If your response is that there's no way you can possibly know that, then you have just said the Bible has no authority.

God was very clear when He wrote His Book. It's not that difficult to understand it. Even though it's good for a pastor to have a mastery of Hebrew, Greek, and all the exegetical nuances, we have to acknowledge that someone with a basic secondary school education can comprehend the English Bible pretty well. Now, don't mistake this to mean you can neglect your study of Greek and Hebrew, because part of understanding the original meaning of a text has to do with knowing how to correctly interpret the original languages.

So use your Greek and Hebrew knowledge to show the authorial intent and the meaning of a passage, but don't use it so much that the sermon becomes a mere academic exercise. Instead, teach your people how to get the authorial intent so they can benefit as fully as possible from their reading of the Bible.

Here's an illustration you might find helpful: Let's say I call a florist and order a dozen roses to be delivered to my wife as a symbol of her meaning the world to me. The deliveryman then takes those roses, shows up at my house, and knocks on the door. When my wife opens the door, the deliveryman says, "Hello, these roses are from Rick." Imagine she replies, "Oh, thank you, but what do they mean?" The man then says, "The message he's trying to send is that you're a thorny pain, you fade in the midday sun, and you smell good in the morning, but you give off a stench at night."

Who is it that determines what the roses mean—the giver, or the deliveryman? The giver, of course. Likewise, your job as a preacher is not to provide your listeners with a "What does this mean to me?" interpretation of God's Word. Rather, you are to communicate the authorial intent. And when you do, then your preaching will be indisputable.

Informational Preaching

Data Necessary for Understanding

The second *I* of life-changing preaching is *informational preaching*. This is the teaching part of the pastor's role, and by this I mean information is the salient data necessary to understand the ancient text in a contemporary context. If you look at the words used in the New Testament to speak of preaching, you'll learn that these terms are predominantly used of evangelism.

When you read through the book of Acts, you see that preaching is a proclamation that leads to a presentation of the gospel. The apostle Paul said, "Woe is me if I do not preach the gospel" (1 Corinthians 9:16). We should always include the gospel in our preaching. I understand that the gospel is not in every text, but the gospel should be in every sermon. Don't shoehorn the gospel in places that it's not, but strive to teach in a manner that eventually leads to an opportunity to present the gospel.

We should give our people information that reveals the beauty of the good news, and this informational preaching can only come from being well-studied. Most of what we do as expositors is akin to what the New Testament calls "teaching." It is the provision of information that comes from Scripture. It informs, instructs, enlightens. Life-changing preaching includes teaching the listener something unknown before. Or, something unclear that becomes lucid.

Important Preaching

Application and Implications

The third *I* of life-changing preaching is *important preaching*. If you want to deliver a life-changing sermon, then it needs to be an important sermon. Importance is conveyed when the sermon is relevant, and relevance is achieved when application and implication are made.

At this point you may be asking, "What is the difference between application and implication?"

Let me explain the distinction through an example. I was over at a friend's house when an incident occurred at the dinner table and my friend had to deal with his kids. I respected this man and wanted to learn from how he handled his children. When I walked away from that encounter, I found myself applying certain implications. I wasn't going to do exactly what he did, because my family context varied from his. But seeing how he applied certain biblical principles to his children helped me to discover implications that were different yet based on the same principles.

If you're too specific in your sermon application, then you will rob your people of the opportunity to be convicted by the Holy Spirit's implications. For example, if you're preaching on self-control and you say, "Hey, do you love cinnamon rolls? The next time you have one, I want you to get all the way down to the last bite and then don't eat it—just stare at it." People might respond, "I get it—I can develop better self-control by not eating everything I want to eat." But if your listener is lactose intolerant, he'll say, "Cinnamon rolls have dairy product in them, so I guess the message doesn't quite apply to me." You see, application is a great tool for the preacher, but it needs to be used sparingly and wisely.

If you explain with clarity the original contextual meaning of a biblical text, it will implicate your people in such a way that they say, "I see where the Lord would have me apply that principle." As a result, they're not stuck with the specific applications you gave at the end of the sermon, but there is freedom for the Holy Spirit to work in their hearts however He wishes.

Does this mean you should never provide applications? Absolutely not. However, you are on safer and more helpful ground when you explain the text in such a manner that your hearers are implicated by what it says, for the Holy Spirit who wrote the Scriptures works in the lives and the hearts of those who are hearing it. If you properly preach the text, your people will learn how to figure out the authorial intent and the implications for their own lives. Therefore, you want to apply sparingly yet implicate constantly.

Insightful Preaching

Explanation that Generates Clarity

The fourth *I* of life-changing preaching is *insightful preaching*. Insight is achieved by an explanation that increases understanding and generates clarity. It produces an "aha moment" in which listeners say, "I've read that before, but I've never seen that." However, you don't want to read too much into a passage and have people say, "I've read that before and I see what you're saying, but I don't think I'll ever see that again." Give insight, but don't resort to overstating the obvious and employing the preaching technique, "Weak point, yell here!"

An example of insightful preaching is taking a phrase like "As Jesus was about to go up to Jerusalem…" (Matthew 20:17) and instead of stating the obvious that can be gleaned from a first reading of the text, you provide a noteworthy detail. You say, "Jericho is so many feet below Jerusalem. It's a fourteen-mile climb from Jericho to Jerusalem, and that's what is meant when the text says Jesus was about to 'go up.'" It's information like this that enhances your listeners' understanding of what's happening.

Interesting Preaching

Arouses Curiosity, Gets Attention, and Provokes Thought

The fifth *I* of life-changing preaching is *interesting preaching*. All preachers can be self-indicted on this point, but for sermons to have impact, they have to be riveting. And interest is created and maintained by preaching that arouses curiosity, gets attention, and provokes thought. If you're going to be boring, pursue another calling, because preaching should never be boring.

When I was 18, I drove from Tennessee to California with a friend. During our cross-country trip we stopped at the Grand Canyon. It was my first visit, and I was completely overwhelmed by what I saw. I wanted to get the full experience of this majestic wonder, so I boarded a tour-guided tram. The guide, in a detached, monotone voice, said, "There's the rock that looks like an alligator. We call that formation 'The Alligator.' The canyon is three thousand feet deep here, and at the bottom you'll see the Colorado River, which is carrying silt." The entire time he was talking I was thinking, *Why does he sound so bored? Everything we're looking at is so remarkable!* Evidently the guide was so used to the beauty that it no longer amazed him. And that affected his presentation. John Piper, in his book *The Supremacy of God in Preaching*, made this observation: "A bored and unenthusiastic tour guide in the Alps contradicts and dishonors the majesty of the mountains."[4]

As preachers we must heed that critique. We need to be interesting, and our listeners will find us more fascinating when we are personally captivated by the text. One of the practical ways to keep your audience's interest is by not using canned illustrations. When you start giving an illustration, you don't want the people in your church to think, *Yeah, I've heard that one before.* Instead, put some thought into your preparation and come up with original illustrations. The best ways to find quality sermon illustrations is by doing a lot of reading and being observant of the world around you. Be enamored with your text and be creative with your illustrations, and you will retain your people's attention.

Intense Preaching

Creating Urgency by Preaching with Passion

The sixth *I* of life-changing preaching is *intense preaching.* Intensity is creating urgency by preaching with passion. I love how Alex Montoya explains this: "I am passionate because God's Word makes me so, because man's condition demands it, and ultimately because the nature of preaching deserves it."[5]

Now, when it comes to passion, I'm not talking about turning up the volume, because if everything is emphasized, then nothing is emphasized. Consider the range of passion that you show in your own personal communication. Your son scores his first basket, and you yell at the top of your lungs. But there's also the whisper on your wedding anniversary, when you're holding your wife's hand during a candlelit dinner and you say, "Sweetheart, I love you."

Don't resort to an artificial passion.
The passion will come when you are excited about the text
and you genuinely care about your listeners.

In both situations, you express passion. And if you faithfully follow the nuances of the biblical text, it will demand both the emphatic and quieter expressions of passion. If you find yourself inclined to be too vocal, learn

THE ART OF CRAFTING A LIFE-CHANGING SERMON 167

to develop a subtle demonstration of passion. And if you tend to be too calm and reserved, then work on ramping up your energy levels.

Whatever you do, don't resort to an artificial passion. The passion will come when you are excited about the text and you genuinely care about your listeners. And in the midst of all this, you must be natural and let whatever personality God has given you be manifest in your preaching.

Imperatival Preaching

Commands and Responses

The seventh *I* of life-changing preaching is *imperatival preaching*. Your preaching must find the imperative voice that demands a response. Paul told Timothy, "Prescribe and teach these things" (1 Timothy 4:11). Preachers are not to suggest or instruct on their own initiative. Rather, they are to declare what the Lord has commanded. For you to be faithful to the apostolic mandate, your sermon must find its way to the imperative voice.

Sadly, some preachers read, "Thou shall not commit adultery," and then say, "Yeah, it's probably a good idea for you not to commit adultery. You will end up hurting your spouse. I hope you don't do it." But that's not what God meant when He said, "Thou shall not commit adultery." God was not offering a suggestion. He was prescribing a command, and as His ambassadors we are to do the same.

Yet we must also preach imperatively with kindness and grace. "The Lord's bond-servant must not be quarrelsome, but be kind to all, able to teach, patient when wronged, with gentleness correcting those who are in opposition" (2 Timothy 2:24-25). Sometimes we can become mean, old, angry preachers who just bark out commands instead of being shepherds who lead our sheep to fairer lands of obedience. Remember that the shepherd's crook has two functions—the curved hook at one end that helps to coddle the sheep back into the fold, and the rod portion that helps to discipline those who go astray.

Impossible Preaching

Communicates the Need of God's Sanctifying Work

The eighth *I* of life-changing preaching is *impossible preaching*. This kind of preaching communicates a righteousness that is not attainable without the regenerating and sanctifying work of God. If people can do what we say by their own efforts, we have not preached faithfully because obedience, justification, and sanctification are impossible without the enabling power of the Spirit of God. There is a drastic difference between genuine heart change and behavior modification.

To illustrate, there are religions that do nothing more than shape a person's external behaviors with no change taking place in the heart. The same is true of psychology—it teaches how to condition people to act in specific ways without bringing about true, internal transformation. Only a magnificent vision of a glorified God who sent His Son to die for wretched sinners can change a heart of stone into a heart of flesh. Impossible preaching challenges the audience to be and to do what they are not and cannot be. It casts a vision, gives hope, and connects to the divine by saying, "Your hope is only in Christ. Now turn to Him, trust Him, and obey Him."

This change, biblically speaking, involves both God's sovereign intervention and man's responsibility. In Philippians 2:12, Paul wrote, "Work out your salvation with fear and trembling." That is a command that calls for effort on the part of the Christian. Then Paul mentions God's part: "For it is God who is at work in you, both to will and to work for His good pleasure" (verse 13).

Paul states the same principle in Colossians 1:29: "For this purpose also I labor." If the verse ended there, I'd be very discouraged because I know I'm not capable of good. But thankfully, the verse doesn't end there: "For this purpose also I labor, striving according to His power, which mightily works within me." In your preaching, you call people to labor and trust that God will work mightily within them. We don't know exactly how this works out, but we are to call people to depend on, pray to, and lean on the Holy Spirit, who causes them to change, causes them to have different affections, causes them to have different motivations, and causes them to take different actions. If you want your preaching to be life-changing, it needs to be impossible preaching.

Invitational Preaching

Inviting Listeners to Make a Decision

The ninth *I* of life-changing preaching is *invitational preaching*. This entails provoking people to make a decision about their justification or sanctification in Christ. The apostle Paul reinforces this in 1 Corinthians 9:16: "Woe is me if I do not preach the gospel." Do you know what Paul was saying? By using the word "woe," he meant, "Let me be cursed and damned if I don't preach and proclaim the gospel."

When you preach, you must always assume there are unbelievers in your audience. If there aren't, then the believers in your congregation will be edified by hearing the gospel again. On a personal note, I challenge you to examine yourself against the teaching of Matthew 7:13-29. This passage reveals there will be people who make it all the way to the judgment seat of Christ thinking they're right with God. They will exclaim, "Lord, didn't we do all these things in Your name?" The Lord will say in return, "I never knew you; depart from Me" (verse 23).

Are you too proud to beg for people to come to Christ?

That leads me to bring up a point about giving invitations after a service. When I first came to Grace Community Church, I was encouraged to hear how Pastor MacArthur concluded a service. He tells everyone in the congregation, "The prayer room is up front to my right. If you want to talk to someone about a relationship with Christ, we have men and women who are waiting for you." Now, I admit that the first few times I heard that, I thought, *No one's going to get saved that way. What are you thinking? Do you know how much God needs your help to get them into the prayer room?*

But that's carnal thinking—God doesn't need our help. We are to invite people with truth that affects the emotions, not emotional appeals through which we hope to give them the truth. Be cautious about how you handle your public invitations, yet be sure that your preaching is invitational.

Integral Preaching

Avoiding Hypocrisy and Inaccuracy

The tenth and final *I* of life-changing preaching is *integral preaching*. The message must be integrated into the messenger's life, and he ought to be a model of what he's proclaiming. The preacher must experience the conviction of working through a text all week, having it pierce his heart, and getting up Sunday morning thinking, *I am undone. I'm going to tell people to be what I'm not.* If your message isn't affecting you, then you have reason to be concerned. Our sermons must change us because preaching without integrity makes us hypocrites; and the two greatest threats to effective preaching are hypocrisy and inaccuracy. Have integrity and be faithful not only in how you preach a text, but in how you apply that text to your own life.

An Example of Inaccuracy

Now that we've looked at the ten *I*'s of life-changing preaching, I want to reinforce once again the importance of finding the authorial intent in a text. Let me put it this way: Suppose you're teaching through the Gospel of Matthew. You preach your way through the genealogy, the Christmas story, and the ministry of John the Baptist. Then you get to Matthew chapter 4, which recounts Jesus' temptation, and you preach a series on how to fight temptation. And you're delighted because the congregation is responding positively.

However, the problem is that Matthew didn't write chapter 4 with the intent that it serve as a guide to fighting temptation. As he was writing, he didn't think, *Since I've provided three chapters of Messianic Christology, I need to add a practical chapter on how to conquer sin.* The authorial intent of Matthew 4 is to fortify the truth that Jesus is the Savior who was tempted in every way like us and yet did not sin.

The application and implication of the wilderness temptations are, "Hallelujah, what a Savior," not a behavior modification plan. Does that mean that you can't include some applications for enduring in the midst of temptation? No, you can preach that because we are called to imitate Christ. However, that's a collateral subordinate application. If you want to preach in a way that is faithful to the Word and changes lives, you must preach the intent of the text and provide an opportunity for your people to be implicated by it.

A Final Impression

Earlier, I quoted this statement about preaching that came from Jonathan Edwards: "The main benefit that is obtained by preaching is by impression made upon the mind in the time of it, and not by the effect that arises afterwards by a remembrance of what was delivered."[6] Is Edwards saying that a sermon should never be remembered? Of course that's not his intention, for he printed his sermons for people to have, to read, and to remember. What he's saying is that something unique occurs when the people of God come under the preacher's leadership, passion, personality, giftedness, study, exegesis, and experience in order to hear the message that God has perfectly ordained for that moment. Those who hear biblical preaching will walk away saying, "What a God and what a gospel."

Your people must see you as a man of the Book, a man who loves the Scriptures and is dedicated to communicating the authorial intent of the text every single week. Their impression must be that you believe that the Bible is the absolute source of authority and your mission is to explain it faithfully. With that in mind, commit yourself to doing what it takes to preach well-crafted sermons that will change people's lives.

PRAYER

Father, give us grace to study and to proclaim Your Word
in a way that's accurate and that portrays Your intention.
We ask for grace to experience the preaching moment that
Edwards wrote of, where for that allotted time, people sit
suspended between heaven and earth with a gaze toward
You, the living Savior. Encourage us through our interaction with Your truth and implicate us for our own
application. In Jesus' name, Amen.

Preaching as a Dying Man to Dying Men

"We proclaim Him, admonishing every man
and teaching every man with all wisdom,
so that we may present every man complete in Christ."

Colossians 1:28

10

PREACHING AS A DYING
MAN TO DYING MEN[1]

Alex Montoya

Shepherds' Conference 2012

Selected Scriptures

In 2 Timothy 4:1-4, Paul exhorted Timothy,

> I solemnly charge you in the presence of God and of Christ
> Jesus, who is to judge the living and the dead, and by His
> appearing and His kingdom: preach the word; be ready in
> season and out of season; reprove, rebuke, exhort, with great
> patience and instruction. For the time will come when they
> will not endure sound doctrine; but wanting to have their ears
> tickled, they will accumulate for themselves teachers in accor-
> dance to their own desires, and will turn away their ears from
> the truth and will turn aside to myths.

These are solemn words that impress upon preachers and teachers the
urgency of declaring God's Word. As preachers, it must be our ambition
to take God's Word and proclaim it verse by verse and chapter by chapter.
Yet we may erroneously think of exposition as an end in itself, but preaching is really a means to an end. The purpose of proclaiming the Bible is so
that individuals might repent of their sins, come to saving faith, and be

transformed into the image of Christ. Paul taught this truth in Colossians 1:28: "We proclaim Him, admonishing every man and teaching every man with all wisdom, so that we may present every man complete in Christ." The purpose of ministry, then, is creating disciples of Christ, and preaching is a means to that end. How do we preach with this vision in mind? How do we preach, as Richard Baxter said, "as a dying man to dying men"?[2] In this chapter we will examine certain features that must characterize our preaching so that it may achieve this purpose.

Errors to Avoid

Before we look at these features, we must first recognize the types of major errors that can arise in our preaching. There are six I would like to highlight.

The Long Sermon

The first error we need to avoid is the long sermon. Some preachers have the notion that longer is better—that somehow the length of the sermon also determines its quality. I was having dinner a few years ago with a pastor and his wife, and I asked him, "What are you preaching on tomorrow?" He responded, "I'm preaching on John chapter six." I said, "Oh, what portion of the chapter are you preaching?" He said, "I'm preaching the whole chapter," and his wife exclaimed, "Oh no!" Your people may be saying the same thing if you're preaching long sermons. Longer is not necessarily better because you need to be an awfully great communicator to hold the attention of your listeners for an extended period of time.

The Dump Truck Sermon

A second error we must steer clear of is the dump truck sermon. This is when the preacher spends 20 to 30 hours a week in exegetical studies, and then backs up the truck on Sunday morning and dumps large quantities of data onto the people of God. More is not always better. An example of this is eating a steak dinner. An eight-ounce fillet mignon is a great piece of meat. Maybe if you're a little bit of a glutton, you enjoy a twelve-ounce slab. However, a fourteen-pound fillet mignon is just too much. Similarly, we don't want to overload our people and assume they can handle large quantities of information.

The Sausage Sermon

Third, we should not preach sausage sermons. These are sermons in which you just continue the exposition from the exact point where you left off the previous week. You'll go for 40, 50, or 60 minutes and when your time is up, you cut it off just like you cut sausage. You never introduce or conclude; you just continue on. This approach doesn't usually go as well as one would like it to go.

The Deep Sermon

The fourth error to avoid is the deep sermon, and by this I mean too complex. Some preachers spend large quantities of their teaching time discussing the original Hebrew and Greek texts and other academic details.

I once had a discussion with a pastor who received a poem from one of his church members. The two-page poem was beautifully written and criticized the pastor's preaching. The man was livid and upset. I read through the poem and said, "This person is doing you a favor. Normally when folks don't like your preaching they don't write you a poem. But this individual is letting you know that you're going so deep in your preaching that she can't make heads or tails out of it."

Sometimes we're so deep that no one knows what we're talking about. We've forgotten that clarity is important when we preach.

The Nowhere Sermon

A fifth error to avoid is the nowhere sermon. In the San Gabriel Mountains near Los Angeles there is a bridge called the Bridge to Nowhere. It spans more than 100 feet above a large crevice and goes absolutely nowhere; ironically, it was built to go nowhere. Sometimes our sermons are like that bridge—they go nowhere. The preacher ends up just occupying a space of time because there's no real purpose in the sermon. Some may attempt to defend themselves by saying, "I don't need a purpose because I'm just going through a book of the Bible." But the reality is that each book has a purpose, and so must your sermons.

> The Bible is the most exciting book
> that has ever and will ever exist, and you are
> to preach it effectively and passionately.

The Boring Sermon

The sixth and ultimate error made in preaching is the boring sermon. Some men are under the impression that boring somehow equates to holiness. The more boring a sermon is in its delivery, the more holy it is. On the contrary, as a preacher, for you to preach a boring sermon is a great sin. Preachers are entrusted with the oracles of God. The Bible is the most exciting book that has ever and will ever exist, and you are to preach it effectively and passionately. You must preach with great fire and energy.

That leads us to the first characteristic that must mark our preaching if we wish to preach as a dying man to dying men.

What It Takes to Preach with Passion

Jerry Vines describes passion in preaching in this way: "We need a return to heart preaching. Perhaps some would use other terminology. Perhaps you would prefer the term 'sincere.' Or maybe you like the word 'earnest.' Whatever you choose to call it, we desperately need it."[3] Martyn Lloyd-Jones, in his wonderful book *Preaching & Preachers*, stressed passion in this way:

> This element of pathos and of emotion is, to me, a very vital one. It has been so seriously lacking in the present century, and perhaps especially among Reformed people. We tend to lose our balance and to become over-intellectual, indeed almost to despise the element of feeling and emotion. We are such learned men, we have such a great grasp of the truth, that we tend to despise feeling. The common herd, we feel, are emotional and sentimental, but they have no understanding![4]

Passion in preaching is the power, the drive, the energy, and the life in the delivery of the sermon. Without passion the sermon becomes just a lecture, an address, a moral speech; and God is not calling us to that. God calls us to preach fervent sermons that declare the unsearchable riches of Christ.

John Broadus, an earnest proponent of expository preaching, wrote, "The chief requisite to an energetic style is an energetic nature. There must be vigorous thinking, earnest if not passionate feeling, and the determined purpose to accomplish some object, or the man's style will have no true, exalted energy."[5] Charles Spurgeon illustrated passion in preaching in *Lectures to My Students* in this way: "We must regard the people as the wood and the sacrifice, well wetted a second and a third time by the care of the week, upon which, like the prophet, we must pray down the fire from heaven. A dull minister creates a dull audience."[6]

Lloyd-Jones reinforced this idea when he said,

> I would say that a "dull preacher" is a contradiction in terms; if he is dull he is not a preacher. He may stand in a pulpit and talk, but he is certainly not a preacher. With the grand theme and message of the Bible dullness is impossible. This is the most interesting, the most thrilling, the most absorbing subject in the universe; and the idea that this can be presented in a dull manner makes me seriously doubt whether the men who are guilty of this dullness have ever really understood the doctrine they claim to believe, and which they advocate. We often betray ourselves by our manner.[7]

Finally, W.A. Criswell, the great Baptist pastor and preacher, said the following about passion in preaching:

> You cannot read the New Testament without sensing that the preachers were electrified by the power of the gospel and swept off their feet by the wonder of the great revelation which had been committed to their trust. There is something wrong if a man charged with the greatest news in the world can be listless and frigid and dull. Who is going to believe that the glad tidings brought by the preacher means literally more than anything else on earth if they are presented with no verve or fire or attack, or if the man himself is apathetic, uninspired, afflicted

with spiritual coma in unsaying by his attitude what he says in words.[8]

These remarks are convicting because we can be dull and boring in the pulpit. God is calling us to preach with great passion and great energy. Now sometimes people who hear me teach on passion in preaching respond by saying, "Montoya, you're Hispanic. You're just passionate by nature. I, however, am not like that."

But passion is not a matter of ethnicity! I want to encourage you today to go through a metamorphosis. I'm not talking about going through a ritual or some mystical act, but simply committing yourself to developing an energetic nature. As a teacher and preacher of God's Word you must learn to develop passion in your heart, your soul, and your life.

With that in mind, I'd like to identify five ways you can bring more passion into your preaching.

Preach with Spiritual Power

The first way to preach with passion is to preach with spiritual power. The English word *enthusiastic* comes from a combination of two Greek words that mean "to be in God" or "God to be in you." To be enthusiastic means to be filled with all that God is. For us to preach with great passion we must be dependent on spiritual power. We must be energized and empowered by God Himself so that the message we preach is coming from Him.

This cannot be artificially produced—it has to be something that becomes part of our nature. To learn to preach with spiritual power, we need to develop contrition of the soul and be men who are deeply underneath the shadow and view of God. We must know that we're simply sinners saved by grace. The great Reformer Martin Luther prayed, "O Lord God, dear Father in heaven, I am indeed unworthy of the office and ministry in which I am to make Thy glory and to nurture and to serve this congregation."[9]

Are you overwhelmed with the weight of the calling that God has entrusted to you? Whether it is 5 teenagers or 500 members you meet with on Sunday morning, they're both a gift, and you ought to be overwhelmed by the fact that you are able to stand before them and preach God's Word.

Clean vessels for master's use. Moreover, if we are to preach with spiritual power, we must approach God as clean preachers. How often have we attempted to continue serving in ministry with sins that have not been confessed, sins that have not been taken care of? We should understand that there can be no fire, no passion, no divine energy if we are before God with unclean hands and an impure heart. You may not be the most learned preacher or the most gilded vessel in the cupboard. In fact, you may be a cracked vase. But above all, you must be a clean vase. Bring to God a clean vessel, and He will honor your resolve. I would encourage you to determine to never go into the pulpit with unclean hands and an impure heart. Take time to confess sins to ensure that you're always a sincere preacher in the pulpit.

Maintain a deep communion with God. As you examine your dependence on God, remember that preaching with spiritual power comes from deep communion with God. You must spend time in His Word. The Puritan minister Richard Baxter said, "Content not yourselves with being in a state of grace, but be also careful that your graces are kept in vigorous and lively exercise, and that you preach to yourselves the sermons which you study, before you preach them to others."[10] Heed that counsel and let your sermons work in your own heart first before they are delivered to others.

Robert M'Cheyne wrote, "In great measure, according to the purity and perfections of the instruments, will be the success. It is not great talent which God blesses so much as great likeness to Jesus. A holy minister is an awesome weapon in the hand of God."[11] As you know, there are too many examples in the media of ministers who have fallen and disqualified themselves. Resolve today that you will stand and preach as a holy vessel of God.

Learn to worship. Another aspect of generating preaching that is spiritually powerful is learning to worship. The worship services at your church should be designed to not only benefit your people, but also to feed and encourage you. Don't ever think that the sermon is the only important portion of your worship service, because it's not. Every part of the service is significant.

I've attended churches where the preacher thinks that everything before the sermon is preliminary—the opening prayer, the hymns, the special number, and the taking of the offering are all just fillers. That is an erroneous mind-set, for when there's an anthem sung to God, it is worship of God. Therefore, worship God along with your people. When an individual sings before the congregation, it is not simply to buy time for the preacher to get ready. Rather, the intent is to bring glory to God. Let the songs that are sung, the words that are said, and the prayers that are prayed feed your soul so when you get up to preach it's from a soul that has been nourished.

Feed yourself. On a similar note, it is not enough to study in preparation of your preaching; you must also study to feed yourself. Some pastors make the mistake of reading their Bibles only for sermon preparation. But it's important for you to read the Word simply for your own benefit so that out of the fullness of the soul there will be an abundance of power to preach.

Remember your calling and commission. A final element of preaching with spiritual power is knowing that you've been called and commissioned by God. This awareness must cause you to rely on God completely and marvel in the wonderful task that He has set before you. I constantly thank the Lord for calling me into ministry. I can't think of anything else that I would rather do. The explanation behind such commitment is the knowledge that God has mandated me to preach. Therefore, I can't resign, I can't retire, and I can't change my calling until the Commander-in-Chief gives me orders to do so.

Ministry is not a profession. It is a call given by God. Be one who preaches with passion by learning to preach with spiritual power.

Preach with Conviction

The second way to preach with passion is to preach with conviction. Men hold opinions, but convictions hold the man. Convictions are spiritual instincts that drive you to action regardless of the circumstances. You can't preach with great passion unless you develop deep convictions.

Trust the Word of God. The Book that we preach from is the inspired

Word of God. Thus, it is without error from cover to cover. This truth was reaffirmed in my life when I took a class in seminary called New Testament Introduction. The course was taught by a beloved professor, Dr. Robert Thomas, who had a reputation for being ruthless as an instructor. He was the sweetest little man who ever slit a throat and scuttled a ship. He was a nice professor, yet his class was extremely difficult because of the large quantities of assigned reading and memorization. In his class we learned about the liberalism that attempts to deny the authority of God's Word through critical methodology. There was so much information for us to remember that many of us came out of the class paralyzed with fear. I remember leaving that class not being able to remember many of the details, but knowing confidently one thing: that the Bible is the inherent, infallible, God-breathed Word.

Convictions fuel passion, and they are cultivated when you trust the perfect and unbreakable Word of God. Therefore, if you're going to preach with the great conviction, you need to preach what the text says. When the preacher studies the text by utilizing and applying sound exegetical tools, the result is the identification of the main point of the text. Consequently, that main point becomes the focal point of your sermon. When you go through a text and the heart of that text becomes clear, you can get excited about preaching it because you are preaching what God intended you to preach.

However, you have to be careful about letting your exegetical studies spill over into your preaching. Every now and then my wife will ask me, "What are you preaching on this Sunday?" We have a standing joke where I reply, "I'm thinking about preaching on the sixteen implications of the iota subscript." She replies, "Wow, it's going to be deep." Unfortunately, that's the way some ministers really do preach. If you are guilty of preaching technical material that doesn't really matter in your people's lives, then how can you expect your people get excited about what you're saying?

Address the people's needs. When it comes to ministering to the people in your church, God hasn't asked you to write exegetical commentaries for them. He's commanded you to preach sermons that help them understand God's Word and how it meets their needs. I understand that every word in the Bible is inspired, but I can assure you that when the believers in Rome had the opening line of Paul's letter read to them—"Paul, a bond servant of Christ Jesus called as an apostle"—they did not sit through 15 sermons expounding on the name *Paul*. The preacher must give his people content they can meditate upon and use in their lives.

Be diligent. If you're going to preach with great conviction, then you must be zealous in preparing for the task. Follow Paul's mandate to Timothy in 2 Timothy 2:15: "Be diligent to present yourself approved to God as a workman who does not need to be ashamed, accurately handling the word of truth." Commit yourself to understanding and rightly dividing God's truth. If you need more training, there are seminaries that can help you. Don't reject crucial preparation for ministry by circumventing the seminaries or your personal study of God's Word, because there are no shortcuts to being a great preacher.

**If your sermon doesn't excite you,
how is it going to excite anyone else?**

Experience the text. Finally, if you're going to preach with conviction, you need to gain an experiential understanding of the text. I try to make sure every sermon I preach keeps me awake on Saturday nights because I can hardly wait to preach it. If your sermon doesn't keep you awake at night, maybe it's not worth preaching. If it doesn't excite you, how is it going to excite anyone else?

The modern world persuades us to be apathetic, to lack convictions and standards, to be spineless preachers. But we are called to take a stand and preach with powerful conviction. When we do, we'll find ourselves preaching with great passion.

Preach with Compassion

The third way to preach with passion is to preach with compassion. It's been said, "To love to preach is one thing. To love those to whom we preach is another."[12] Some ministers love to preach, yet they don't love the people whom they preach to. If that's the case for you, then you're not a preacher. Ministers are entrusted by God to tend and love the flock. That's why Jesus said to Peter, "Peter, tend My lambs" (John 21:15). Peter's commission was to love and care for God's people.

Love is an attitude that often takes effort to develop because some church members are difficult to love; and yet they're the ones most in need of love. I've been asked, "How do you respond to people when they tell you that you preached a great sermon?" My response is, "Did I help you?" If I've helped someone, then I've succeeded in preaching with compassion. Even with what I've written in this chapter my intent is to help you. If I can contribute to you becoming a better teacher and preacher, then I have accomplished my task. I love you and want you to succeed in your ministry.

Preach to convert. A big part of preaching with compassion is preaching with a heart for converting people to Christ. As you preach, always be in love with bringing lost souls to Christ. You can also preach to correct the ignorant. There are people out there who do not know up from down. It's interesting to note that the apostle Paul addressed the Galatians as "you foolish Galatians" (Galatians 3:1). The apostle corrected this church out of deep care and love for them. Still another way to show compassion is by reproving the wayward. There are some people who are going the wrong way, and you need to exhort them to turn around. I'm reminded of the deacon who came up to the pastor, who had been preaching to reprove, and said, "Pastor, I think you're stroking the cat the wrong way." The pastor replied, "Well, turn the cat around."

Preach to heal. Not only are we to correct the ignorant and reprove the wayward, we are also to preach to heal the broken. While it's true that we are called to preach in a way that convicts, we must also remember that there are people who are already broken. We need to preach so that we can bring healing to the wounded.

Preach to teach. A compassionate preacher is one who keeps the teaching simple so people will learn. J. Vernon McGee was such a preacher. Though he is now with the Lord, his sermons are still broadcasted all around the world. McGee was known for saying, "Place the cookies on the lower shelf." We need to preach simple sermons, because clarity is the chief requisite in oratory. If people don't understand what you are saying, then you are wasting their time.

Preach to inspire. Another way to show compassion is by preaching to inspire the weary. Many of our people live one day at a time. They come every Sunday with one cry: "Pastor, give me hope for one more day." There's an elderly woman who comes to our church and sits in the back and sneaks in and out every Sunday. Although I do not know her well, I do know that she's very sick and I know she comes with this prayer: "Give me hope for one more week." When you preach, be aware that there are people who are knocking on the gates of heaven and they need hope for one more day.

Preach to yourself first. You might be asking, "How do you stir up compassion?" I don't have an easy answer for you, but here is what I recommend: First, study your own heart and preach to yourself. Every sermon I preach, I preach first to myself. I know who I am, I know what I need, and I know that I'm like the rest of humanity. You are cut from the same cloth as your congregation, so you too need to be corrected, inspired, and encouraged. So start by preaching to yourself.

Know your congregation. Some pastors are afraid to live among their people. They want to be as far away from their people as possible and don't want to be involved in their lives. But if we're going to preach with compassion, we need to live among our people. How can you gain compassion for the people in your church if you don't know who they are? Get out there and live among them. Interact with them, and make them yours.

How are you going to win people to the Lord or help them if you avoid them? You have to be with your people. As you live among them, you will grow in your love and compassion for them. Do not fall into the trap of thinking that you can hide from the people and still be an effective preacher, because you can't. Instead, learn to listen to their groaning and cries. Preach with a moist eye, and keep your heart sensitive before God. Then you will learn what it means to preach with compassion.

Preach with Authority

The fourth way to preach with passion is to preach with authority. Timothy was given the charge, "Preach the word" (2 Timothy 4:2). Likewise, God commands all preachers to faithfully preach the Word with great influence. Don't misinterpret this as permission to be an authoritarian or egocentric pulpiteer. Rather, this is a commission to come before the people of God—whether through a sermon or a simple interaction with one soul—and say to them, "Thus says the Lord." We are not called to give suggestions, opinions, or make frivolous remarks. Instead, our mandate is to speak on behalf of God.

Believe what you preach and fulfill your commission. From a practical standpoint, how do you come to preach with authority? First, you need to believe what you preach. The apostle Paul wrote, "We also believe, therefore we also speak" (2 Corinthians 4:13). You must follow the example of the apostle and speak what you believe. You preach with authority when you preach as one who believes.

Second, to preach with authority means you speak as an ambassador. Martyn Lloyd-Jones wrote,

> The preacher should never be apologetic, he should never give the impression that he is speaking by their leave as it were; he should not be tentatively putting forward certain suggestions and ideas. This is not to be his attitude at all. He is a man, who is there to "declare" certain things; he is a man under commission and under authority. He is an ambassador, and he should be aware of his authority. He should always know that he comes to the congregation as a sent messenger.[13]

You are a sent messenger; therefore, when you execute your ministry, you execute it as an ambassador. Many churches today are in total disarray with people who are in auto-rebellion against God, His authority, and His Word because there are preachers who have lost their valor.

As preachers, we cannot be cowards. For example, I seek out members of my congregation who haven't attended church for a lengthy period of time. I show up at their house, knock on the door, and when the door opens, I say, "Hi, I've come to see if everything is okay." Typically these visits are difficult because they involve me calling someone to repentance, but I make them because I am a commissioned ambassador of God.

Every once in a while I'll ask my secretary to set appointments with a list of people who are having difficulties. As soon as she starts calling, the responses are, "What does he want? Well, tell him I can't." But you don't stop pursuing those who have wandered because as an overseer, that is part of your job description. You are expected to shepherd the flock of God with loving authority.

Showing this kind of authority doesn't always come naturally. I found this out during the third year of my pastorate at the same church I've been serving now for 40-plus years. There was an uprising in the church because some of the leaders wanted to fire me. There were some who didn't like the idea that I wanted the people to live by God's Word. As soon as I heard about their plan, I got up in the pulpit the next Sunday morning and said, "I've heard that some of you are thinking of firing me, but I want to let you know that you're not going to do that." I continued, "I'm here for the long haul, and I'm going to bury you." Back in those days, I was in my late twenties and most of the other leaders were older, so I knew I was going to outlast them and officiate their funerals. Now if you know me and my personality, you know that is very unlike me—that kind of authority does not come naturally. However, I do what I need to do because God has called me to shepherd His flock. When I'm in the pulpit, I am no longer Alex Montoya; I am an ambassador who proclaims God's Word with authority.

As a pastor, you are to preach the truth in such a way that people realize it must be obeyed.

Preach as a scholar. If you want to preach with authority, you need to preach as a scholar—as one who knows the Bible well. There is much that I don't know, but there is one thing I absolutely must know: the Bible. I don't know much about basketball, football, or baseball. I don't know anything about celebrities, and my knowledge of pop culture is limited. But ultimately, there's one area in which I need to be an expert, and that is the Scriptures.

Perhaps you know the scores of every game and the stats of every player, but you have not mastered your Bible. As a messenger of God, your time must be consumed with the Bible. When a parishioner asks you a question, you must be ready to give him chapter and verse. Do your homework, and preach with a mastery of the Bible.

Preach as a saint. To preach authoritatively, you should strive to preach as a saint. This simply means to practice what you preach. You can know the Bible thoroughly and you can preach it as an ambassador, but if you're a hypocrite, people will not listen to you. As a pastor, you're living in a fishbowl and everyone is watching you. Make sure you're a clean fish in a bowl with no dirt in it, for a pure life carries with it authority.

Master the art of preaching. If you are to preach with authority, you must speak as a skilled artist. Preaching should be your hobby, and you should master the art of preaching. Churches are dying because preachers can't preach, and they can't preach because they don't bother to put in the effort to preach well.

It's easy for us to think we are good at preaching when the reality is that we're not. Have you read a book on preaching since you finished seminary? Do you listen to your own sermons to see whether they might be homiletically deficient? Do you ask others for advice, or work to perfect your sermons? If a musician wants to be taken seriously, he has to practice playing his instrument hours upon hours. Likewise, if you want to be taken seriously, you need to be a practiced, skilled communicator.

If people are leaving your church and going down the street to a place where heresy is taught, it could be because that preacher has mastered the art of communicating. You shouldn't fault that man; rather, he ought to fault you because you have the truth and yet you don't bother to think about how to properly deliver it. You need to keep working on your preaching ability and perfecting your skills.

When it comes to boring sermons, some pastors might use the excuse, "Well, the people in my church aren't willing to endure deep truth." Or they say, "My congregation is getting soft." But don't assume that reluctance toward deep truth is necessarily the problem. If people are zoning out or falling asleep on you, it may be because of your preaching. You've got to preach in a way that makes people want to listen. Learn to speak as a skilled communicator.

Preach with Urgency

The fifth way to preach with passion is to preach with urgency. David Eby wrote,

> Preaching today is so often passive, apathetic, impotent, soft, spineless and lame. It lacks fervor, heat, and heart. It is

passionless. Preachers must become gospel maniacs. Preachers must become captivated and re-captivated by the Lord
Jesus Christ and the Gospel. No intoxication for the gospel,
no mania for the good news means no fire. No fire means no
power preaching.[14]

You could say that passion is a sanctified madness that is driven by a
deep sense of urgency. When you preach, you need to develop a certain
sense of desperation by always thinking of God's future judgment for
unbelievers. Sin is an enemy of the soul and of God, and the consequence
of sin is eternal torment and judgment. This should provoke you to preach
with urgency. Each time you step into the pulpit, remember that people
are on the verge of dying and going to hell. C.H. Spurgeon wrote, "The
awful and important thoughts of souls being saved by our preaching or left
to perish, to be condemned to hell through our negligence always dwell
upon our spirits."[15] May that be true of you—may you preach with desperation and preach toward a verdict.

A sermon should never be a bridge to nowhere, but instead a persuasive plea for the salvation of souls. Some will criticize this kind of thinking
by saying, "It's not my job to persuade people. That's God's job." My reply
is, "Have you read the Bible? Paul, knowing the terror of the Lord's judgment, said, 'We persuade men'" (2 Corinthians 5:11).

If people aren't changing under your preaching ministry, maybe it's
because you're not expecting them to change. If your preaching is apathetic, lifeless, and lacking passion, then of course nothing will happen.
But if you preach toward a verdict, you'll preach with a sense of urgency
that recognizes your listeners might not have a second chance. The Lord
will bless that kind of preaching.

Making a Statement

I want to conclude on a note of exhortation. In the Orient, when a
man wants to make a statement to the world, he takes gasoline, pours it
on himself, and then lights a match. His consumed life becomes a vivid
and bold declaration.

As a preacher, you can do the same. You can take your Bible, drench yourself in it, light a match, and burn with passion every single Sunday by preaching with great fervency for the glory of God. That's the kind of preaching that is passionate—and that changes lives. We should make it our consuming desire to develop a passionate heart that results in a passionate life for God that results in a passionate preacher who then preaches passionate sermons. There is no reason, there can be no excuse, for the lack of passionate preaching. If we have no definite desire to benefit God's people through the passionate preaching of His Word, then we have no right to ascend into the sacred pulpit to declare the eternal truths found in Scripture. Only a man set aflame by the Word of God should ever enter the pulpit to burn himself out in preaching to change lives and bring eternal glory to God. May you be that man.

PRAYER

Lord, take us and mold us into great preachers for Your honor and Your glory. May we preach the unsearchable riches of Christ with passion, power, and a sense of urgency. Holy and merciful Father, may we look upon this world of ours and may we feel as our Lord Jesus felt towards scattered sheep, afflicted and without a shepherd. Help us to feel deeply about them, to care for them, to yearn for their eternal salvation and spiritual good. God, place Your passion for the world into our hearts so that we can preach Your eternal Word with passion. We ask this in Jesus' name, Amen.

APOLLOS: AN AUTHENTIC MINISTER OF THE GOSPEL

"Being fervent in spirit, he was speaking and
teaching accurately the things concerning Jesus."

ACTS 18:25

11

APOLLOS: AN AUTHENTIC
MINISTER OF THE GOSPEL

Albert Mohler Jr.
Shepherds' Conference 2011

Acts 18:24-28

Faithfulness, steadfastness, and resolute dedication to ministry in the kingdom of God demands models, mentors, and examples. There's a sense in which today's generation is rather reluctant to make this admission. This generation would like to sometimes believe that they can do very well on their own, but this kind of thinking is a recipe for disaster. The Scriptures provide us with many models, and it's important for us to understand their function in our lives. For example, the apostle Paul said, "Be imitators of me, just as I also am of Christ" (1 Corinthians 11:1). The believers in Corinth needed a model, and they had one in the apostle Paul. Along with Paul, there are many positive models whom we want to emulate, but there are also tragic examples that God knows we need to learn from. The Scriptures mention King David, who was described as a man after God's own heart (1 Samuel 13:14), but it also reminds us of Saul, a paranoid and faithless man lurking and brooding in the background, similar to Shakespeare's King Lear or US President Richard Nixon in his last days.

If we want to be faithful until the end, then we're going to need models to follow. I would like to take a look at one of the most neglected figures in the New Testament—I invite you to look with me at Acts 18:24-28 so we can learn from Apollos and his ministry. Let's read together the Word of God:

> Now a Jew named Apollos, an Alexandrian by birth, an eloquent man, came to Ephesus; and he was mighty in the Scriptures. This man had been instructed in the way of the Lord; and being fervent in spirit, he was speaking and teaching accurately the things concerning Jesus, being acquainted only with the baptism of John; and he began to speak out boldly in the synagogue. But when Priscilla and Aquila heard him, they took him aside and explained to him the way of God more accurately. And when he wanted to go across to Achaia, the brethren encouraged him and wrote to the disciples to welcome him; and when he had arrived, he greatly helped those who had believed through grace, for he powerfully refuted the Jews in public, demonstrating by the Scriptures that Jesus was the Christ.

It's a mystery in many ways as to why Apollos is so neglected. He is somewhat of an enigma. In the entire Bible, there are only ten verses that make reference to Apollos, and most of them simply mention his name. Yet in this passage we will witness the things that are said of him that are said of no other character in the New Testament. In this very crucial passage, we learn a great deal about this man and why he should be among our models for ministry.

The Historical Context

The author of our chosen text is the great historian, Luke. In the book of Acts, Luke shares with us details about the embryonic church in its earliest development, as well as the leaders who were important contributors to that growth. Luke teaches us about a time when the gospel is being hammered out in terms of its proclamation, when the church is coming together and learning what it means to be the people of God, and when the Holy Spirit is infusing Christ's church with power and sending it out into the world as a mighty missionary force. In Acts, Luke depicts Christ calling men to serve His church in a way that is absolutely spectacular and unbelievably powerful.

Before continuing with our study of Apollos, we must recognize that Luke's authorial technique in Acts is similar to his approach in the Gospel of Luke. Although the Bible is the inerrant and infallible Word of God, God's glory is demonstrated by His use of men as the authors of sacred Scripture. The Holy Spirit worked within human authors to produce the text of the Word of God. Yet the Spirit didn't use these authors robotically; instead, in His sovereignty, He created each author, He determined the context of each author's experiences, and He formed each author's heart in such a way that it was the Holy Spirit who led the human author to write Scripture.

Viewing Scripture through this prism, we are reminded that Matthew should be understood, at least in part, for the theme of subversion. When we read the Gospel of Matthew, we come to understand that Matthew loves seeing things flipped on their head. Matthew enjoys showing the principalities and the powers—or for that matter, the Pharisees and the Sadducees—get thrown into a rodeo where everything is upside down. Mark, of course, has the feature of urgency as he often used the word "immediately." John, in terms of his Gospel, demonstrates majestic prose that is filled with much irony. And Luke's writings to Theophilus provide an orderly and factual account of the story of Jesus and the church.

As we read the historical narrative of Acts we are susceptible to rushing too quickly over little pieces of embedded language. For instance, chapter 18 begins with Paul leaving Athens and going to Corinth, where he is introduced to Aquila and his wife Priscilla, strategically placed by God in that city for the purpose of ministry. In verse 4 Luke presents Paul as reasoning in the synagogue every Sabbath as his customary missiology, "trying to persuade Jews and Greeks." In verse 5 Luke writes, "When Silas and Timothy came down from Macedonia, Paul began devoting himself completely to the word." If you're going to be a preacher, make sure you're occupied with the Word.

Paul's priority was clear. He was preoccupied with the Word and nothing else. Brother, may it be that when your people find you, they find you preoccupied with the Word. Paul, as our model and mentor, is found devoted to the Word. This holistic commitment harkens back to the earlier chapters in Acts and the need for deacons. This goes right back to the priority of the teaching office in the church. It goes back to the preeminence of the ministry of the Word. Paul was not to be troubled with lesser matters, for he was occupied with the Word.

This ministry of the Word got Paul into trouble and led to hostility from enemies of the truth. We read in Acts 18:6, "When they resisted and blasphemed, [Paul] shook out his garments and said to them," going back to Ezekiel, "Your blood be on your own heads! I am clean. From now on I will go to the Gentiles."[1] Now this is a great turning point in the book of Acts, for from this time forward, Paul's ministry is to the Gentiles.

We come to understand, as the story further progresses, that there's an escalating conflict God was preparing Paul for: "The Lord said to Paul in the night by a vision, 'Do not be afraid any longer, but go on speaking and do not be silent'" (Acts 18:9). Even in the midst of rejection, the apostle is commanded to continue declaring the truth. This, in turn, cultivates more conflict, as we see in Acts 18:12-15:

> While Gallio was proconsul of Achaia, the Jews with one accord rose up against Paul and brought him before the judgment seat, saying, "This man persuades men to worship God contrary to the law." But when Paul was about to open his mouth, Gallio said to the Jews, "If it were a matter of wrong or of vicious crime, O Jews, it would be reasonable for me to put up with you; but if there are questions about words and names and your own law, look after it yourselves; I am unwilling to be a judge of these matters."

Paul demonstrated his faithfulness to do exactly what God called him to do by opening his mouth, but Gallio, when he heard the greatest theological debate imaginable, responded with, "Just words. No intervention for me needed here. No decision or determination from the proconsul is required. Just go off and fiddle with your words."

In this chapter we have a great contrast between Paul, who is preoccupied with the Word, and Gallio, who sees Paul's message as just empty words. This same contrast is very much evident in our world today. There are those who know that the Word of God is that which must occupy us above all, and there are others who think the Bible is just filled with words. This is the background for the story of Apollos.

Introducing Apollos

In Acts 18:24 we are introduced to Apollos with these words: "Now a Jew named Apollos, an Alexandrian by birth, an eloquent man, came to Ephesus." In writing this narrative, Luke makes it a point to highlight Apollos' ethnicity—he was a Jewish man with a Greek name. There's something immediately jarring to the Jewish reader in hearing that a Jewish man had a pagan Greek name. As we continue to read Luke's description we come to realize why this is the case—Apollos was from Alexandria, the first location where the Jewish diaspora resided in the first century. It was also the most important intellectual center of the Mediterranean world, especially after the fall of Athens. Alexandria's culture was defined by its museum and library, which was the greatest library in the ancient world. Because Alexandria was a center of learning and the Jewish people were a people of learning, it was natural for many of the Jewish diaspora to come to Alexandria, for they were drawn to the kind of learning that this city provided. This Hellenistic learning center was Apollos's hometown.

In addition to being the center of ancient pagan knowledge, intellectual activity, and achievement, Alexandria was the city where the Septuagint, the Greek edition of the Old Testament, was translated in the second century BC. As a Jewish boy, Apollos would've been raised in the Alexandrian context of Hellenistic Judaism and trained in the Greek translation of the Holy Scriptures. This was a facility and ability that gave him a tremendous missionary advantage in the Greek culture. This was God's providence at work, overseeing his life to prepare him for future ministry in the Gentile world.

Marks of an Authentic Minister

In addition to these two introductory details concerning Apollos, Luke makes six commendations of Apollos that are rarely said of anyone else in Scripture, and no one else in Scripture has all six of these commendations attributed to him. As we review them, let us consider Apollos as a model to follow.

Eloquent

The first commendation that Luke makes about Apollos is that he was "an eloquent man." That's an important detail to know when you're talking about a figure in the first-century Greco-Roman culture. To be an eloquent man in that historical context is to say Apollos was educated, sophisticated, gifted, and consequential for public meeting.

Eloquence was the ticket into public significance. It was necessary for a public figure to have the ability to make an argument and hold an audience's attention. In Greco-Roman culture, the sign of having an orderly mind was the ability to speak orderly words that were articulated in accordance to the ancient canons of rhetoric.

This, of course, raises a question. You may recall that the apostle Paul said to the Corinthians, "When I came to you, I did not come with lofty words of human wisdom. I did not come to you arguing on the basis of the canons of classical rhetoric in order that my rhetoric would impress you, but rather that the simplicity of the gospel would impress you" (my paraphrase, 1 Corinthians 2:1). As Paul was making his argument against the canons of classical rhetoric, he was still using them. Was Paul being double-minded? No! He was making the point that although ministry is not all about eloquence, it's difficult to be heard if you can't communicate.

In his famed and precious *Lectures to My Students*, Charles Spurgeon spoke about this in terms of the call to ministry. Spurgeon made it clear that if an individual is unable to speak in public, then he is not called to preach.[2] If the last thing you want to do is to get up and speak, preaching is not God's call for your life. If you're worth your salt, you read a text like 1 Corinthians 2:1 and you want to say, "Get out of the way; let's at least make this event a preaching tag team." However, if your temptation is to run into the foyer and bite your nails, you're not called to preach. Yet at the same time we realize that eloquence is not enough. If that were all that had been said about Apollos, it couldn't possibly explain why he had fulfilled such a crucial role in this turning point of church history.

One of the failures of the church today is that eloquence is not encouraged. There are far too many preachers who glory in a lack of eloquence—not because they fear their rhetoric might get in the way of the gospel, but because they just don't want to put in the effort to learn how to speak effectively. A second failure is that there are many leaders who aren't training young men in eloquence. God bless the pastor who looks at a 15-year-old and says, "I want you to make an announcement." I understand that public speaking may be the last thing a kid wants to do, but that's why you're there to guide him.

I recall being in a school gymnasium with a giant swimming pool. Nearby was a father who was teaching his nine-year-old son how to swim. The father leaned over to his son and said, "I want you to know and remember two things: I love you, and you're not going to die." Then I heard a large splash as the boy hit the water, and the father said, "We've got us a swimmer!" A person learns from hands-on experience. Eloquence is developed through experience, and we learn from Luke that Apollos was an eloquent man.

**In the relationship between
a pastor and the congregation, there must be
a level of trust in the preacher's ability
to rightly divide the Word of truth.**

Mighty in the Scriptures

Luke's second commendation of Apollos is that he was "mighty in the Scriptures" (Acts 18:24). Our eyes are drawn to this phrase because this is exactly what we want to be. Luke indicates that Apollos was powerful, dynamic, and at home in the Scriptures. He not only knew the Scriptures but had facility, expertise, and a level of dynamic power in the Scriptures—so much so that when he and the Scriptures came together, the power of

God was shown. It's not enough to be mighty in the Scriptures in terms of your own study; God calls you to be dynamic and show how His Word can take a hold of a congregation.

The pattern we find in the book of Acts is that competence in the Scriptures is necessary if a congregation is going to trust a preacher. In the relationship between a pastor and the congregation, there must be a level of trust in the preacher's ability to rightly divide the Word of Truth. The congregation must know that the preacher is a trustworthy exegete who is a competent interpreter of Scripture. It is expected of the man of God that when he stands behind the pulpit, proper biblical exposition will be the result.

There are far too many pulpits that are simply a piece of furniture because they are not the launching pad for a dynamic preaching ministry. Since exegesis is both an art and a science, ministers must be prepared. That is why Paul told Timothy to study rather than sit in the room and hum a sacred syllable. Timothy needed to study in order to prove himself to be someone who was not ashamed as he rightly divided the Word of Truth (2 Timothy 2:15).

Instructed in the Way of the Lord

Luke's third commendation of Apollos is that he was "instructed in the way of the Lord" (Acts 8:25). The implication is that Apollos was instructed in the Old Testament. His parents must have raised him in the admonition of God. Yet he surpassed that knowledge and came to know the things concerning Jesus as well. It may not be possible to retrace his education down to his mentors, but we should be reminded that the Christian church has been an instructional people from the beginning. The church has always been instructed by the Scriptures. Where you find Christians, you will find instruction. Teaching is absolutely necessary to the Christian faith.

The Christian faith is not passed on by osmosis or by proximity. Rather, it is passed on by the cognitive transmission of biblical truth, which requires an instructor in order for there to be instruction. Many churches today will implement everything into their program except for instruction, and if you happen to find instruction, most likely it isn't instruction from the Scriptures. This is a sad reality because in order to have an Apollos, you need someone who will train him to be competent in the Scriptures, some-one who will instruct him in the way of the Lord.

Fervent in Spirit

The fourth commendation said of Apollos is that he was "fervent in spirit" (Acts 8:25). There are many things we might infer from the phrase "fervent in spirit," which is why biblical exegesis is not about inference. In a situation like this it may be beneficial to let Scripture interpret Scrip-ture. In Romans chapter 12 Paul wrote about the ideal Christian, and in verse 11 he mentioned this specific mark of such a Christian: "Not lagging behind in diligence, fervent in spirit, serving the Lord." Fervency is not about an attitude of excitement but about a zeal for the things of God that is translated into action. To be fervent in spirit is in contrast to being sloth-ful. Where you find a man of God, you will find a man who is working, who is diligent, and who is fervent. He understands what is at stake and is motivated by the power of the gospel to fulfill gospel ministry. Someone who's fervent is always found busy, just like Paul was found occupied with the Word and Apollos was found busy serving the Lord.

In my academic career, I've seen students whom I felt like I wanted to jolt just to make sure they were alive. The minister of the gospel is sup-posed to look alive. He doesn't look alive just because his eyes are open and his chest is moving as he breathes, but because he's diligent in action. Fervency in spirit is clearly demonstrated in the fact that Apollos didn't just wash up in Ephesus. Instead, he was there because of his aspiration to serve the Lord. Every once in a while students tell me, "I can't find a place to serve." My response to them is, "Don't find a place to serve. Find a need and fill it!"

I discovered my call to teach when I was 16 years old. It was a Satur-day night and my father, who was a Sunday school director, came into my room and said, "I'm short a teacher for Sunday morning." He then looked at me and said, "You're going to teach first-grade Sunday school in the morning." He gave me the material and told me to be prepared. I sat down and began to study the Word in a different way than I had ever stud-ied it before. That night I discovered there is a difference between study-ing the Word and studying the Word to teach it.

I was pretty pumped on Sunday morning and I even dressed up for the occasion. I walked into the Sunday school room and it was filled with six-year-olds swarming around like ants looking for a crumb. After I assessed the situation, I asked them to sit down and began to teach. Since that day, there has hardly been a Lord's day when I did not teach. I didn't volunteer; it was foisted upon me, and it turned out to play an instrumental role in me recognizing my calling.

Find a need and fill it. Be fervent in spirit.

Speaking and Teaching Faithfully

Fifth, Luke describes Apollos as someone who "was speaking and teaching accurately the things concerning Jesus" (Acts 18:25). We certainly hope there is some eloquence in us; we certainly want to be found powerful in the Scriptures; we want to be fervent in spirit; but how we must long to be men who speak and teach accurately the things concerning Jesus.

Avoiding heresy isn't merely a decision you can make and thus protect yourself from such a tragedy. There are men who would have never willfully decided, "I'm going to teach heresy" who are currently teaching it. Sometimes the difference between orthodoxy and heresy is so microscopically small that it can be reduced to a diphthong or a vowel. A vowel divided the Roman Empire as it was the difference between saying that Jesus is of a similar substance with the Father, or that He is of the same substance as the Father. That took place in Nicaea in AD 325, where the church came together to hear Athanasius confront the heresy of Arius. It wasn't about getting a sentence wrong. It wasn't about getting a phrase wrong. It wasn't about getting a diphthong or a vowel wrong. It was about an error which meant that the Jesus of Arius was a Jesus who could not save.

Apollos is commended because he "was speaking and teaching accurately the things concerning Jesus." We need to recognize with brokenheartedness that we do not have to look hard to find heresy. Heresy draws an enormous audience and virtually every time it sounds sweet to the ear of the one who does not know the truth. Heresy is a dangerous lure. It's a false gospel that elevates an idol rather than Jesus Christ. Therefore we must understand that it takes work, dedication, theological expertise, doctrinal grounding, and convictional commitment to speak and to teach accurately the things concerning Jesus.

Speaking Boldly

The sixth and final word of commendation is that Apollos is bold (Acts 18:26). We are told that "he...[spoke] boldly in the synagogue." Apollos was audacious and courageous and willing to face the fear of opposition and to conquer it.

I love reading history, especially military history. One of my favorite stories is about General George Patton pressing into Nazi-occupied territory and liberating village after village. He was moving so quickly that he was ahead of his communication lines, and a modern military cannot operate without communication lines. At one point, Patton was riding in a jeep up to the front lines where there were Messerschmitt fighter planes diving down right over the American troops. As the fighter planes were shooting, there was a 17-year-old private on top of a tree putting up a telephone line. Patton, upon seeing him said, "Son, if I only had an army of you. You're not afraid of anything." With a cracking voice the private said, "Yes I am, sir." Patton said, "What are you afraid of?" The boy responded, "You, sir."[3]

Everybody is afraid of something, and that's not a problem. However, an unwillingness to conquer the fear is a problem, for it shows a focus on the self that is unhealthy. As preachers, we must be bold—not because we have confidence in ourselves, but because we have confidence in the One who has called us, confidence in the One who has sent us, and confidence in the One who is worthy. Because of our confidence in the Lord, we can be bold, audacious, and with courage face our fear and conquer it. The preacher must be found doing what he is called to do, especially in the face of opposition.

Teachable and Humble

In addition to Luke's six commendations of Apollos, in Acts 18:25 we are told indirectly that Apollos was a humble and teachable man. Luke writes, "He was speaking and teaching accurately the things concerning Jesus, being acquainted only with the baptism of John." The second half of that verse reveals a serious problem, but one that is understandable considering Apollos's biography. Earlier we saw that he grew up in Alexandria in the context of Hellenistic Judaism, and yet somehow he heard the gospel. However, the gospel he heard was partial—similar to the gospel that was understood by the disciples of John.

It was at this point that Priscilla and Aquila entered the narrative to help Apollos. The Lord sovereignly placed Priscilla and Aquila in Ephesus at the exact moment that Apollos and the church needed them. Luke presents this couple as Paul's friends from Corinth: "After these things he [Paul] left Athens and went to Corinth. And he found a Jew named Aquila, a native of Pontus, having recently come from Italy with his wife Priscilla, because Claudius had commanded all the Jews to leave Rome" (Acts 18:1-2).

This is the couple who "took him [Apollos] aside and explained to him the way of God more accurately" (18:26). This verse is precious to us because here we have an unprecedented model of theological correction in the New Testament. Here we have a man who's described as fervent in spirit, eloquent, competent, and mighty in the Scriptures, and yet he doesn't know everything he needs to know about the gospel. It's possible to be mighty in the Scriptures and to be wrong on a point of doctrine and need correction. In all this, we learn that Apollos was teachable and humble.

The Need for Correction

Priscilla and Aquila heard Apollos and they recognized a problem. They realized that though he taught accurately the things concerning Jesus, when he spoke about baptism, he was left with a baptism of repentance not a baptism that points to regeneration. Apollos didn't have the complete picture, so the couple took him aside—that is to say, they did not confront him publicly. They didn't shame him or embarrass him before the congregation. Instead, in the love of Christ, they taught him the things of God more accurately. We need a church that is filled not only with the likes of Apollos but with the likes of Priscilla and Aquila as well. We desperately need Christians who have the ability to hear what is not accurate and are willing to correct it.

Good intentions are not enough when it comes to gospel ministry. Gospel ministry demands accuracy.

Apollos boldly proclaimed Christ in the synagogue, and in boldness Priscilla and Aquila corrected him. We live in an era in which it is considered a matter of bad etiquette to tell someone he is wrong. In this intellectually demilitarized age, we have declared doctrinal self-surrender. We're not supposed to tell people they're wrong. However, good intentions are not enough when it comes to gospel ministry. Gospel ministry demands accuracy. As a result, we need people like Priscilla and Aquila.

Correcting with Grace

I recall an incident that occurred when I was 26 years old. I was trained in a liberal theological seminary at which I now serve as president. By the grace of God, over the years I had the opportunity to lead this seminary through a process of reformation so that now it stands for the true faith. I was trained by my parents, church, and faithful men who invested in me so that I was saved from the poison of theological liberalism. I had to learn how to listen to discern, but I didn't catch everything. I was taught in seminary that God was an equal-opportunity employer, and thus the office of pastor was said to be open to women as well as men. I had not read a single argument against that, and I picked up that teaching like a virus. One of the men who challenged my thinking on this was the evangelical theologian Carl F.H. Henry. He became a personal mentor, teacher, and friend. I had the opportunity to edit his writings and get to know him as a colleague.

The first time I met Dr. Henry, I was asked to be his host. He wasn't my colleague then, but rather a titanic theological figure. While we were walking across the campus he questioned me on everything from Process Theology to Liberation Theology. He inquired of my views on the inerrancy of Scripture and he was seemingly satisfied with everything he heard. But then he turned to me and asked, "What do you think about women in ministry?" With youthful audacity, I told him what I thought. He simply looked at me and said, "One day, this is going to be a very embarrassing conversation."

After finishing my responsibility to host him, I went to the library. I attempted to find every book I could on the subject, but the resources on biblical manhood and womanhood were scarce. The excellent book *Recovering Biblical Manhood and Womanhood*[4] hadn't been written yet, and the Council of Biblical Manhood and Womanhood had not yet been established. So I started reading the only thing I could find, which was a book by a confused Catholic Charismatic who argued against women serving as priests. The book prompted me to spend the rest of the night ransacking the Scriptures, and it didn't take all that long for me to be persuaded. When I met Dr. Henry the following morning, I told him of my quest and where I ended up. His response was, "Didn't take long, did it?" I said, "No, sir!" This was no small doctrinal issue, but Dr. Henry was gracious to me.

Dr. Henry later asked me to coauthor a work with him. It requires grace and courage to face someone and say, "That's wrong," and then say, "Come with me." That is what Priscilla and Aquila did with Apollos—they confronted him, and then taught him.

What Will Be Said of You?

Whenever Paul referred to Apollos in his writings, he always did so with positive comments. For example, he wrote, "I planted. Apollos watered" (1 Corinthians 3:6). Toward the end of 1 Corinthians we read that Paul encouraged Apollos to visit the Christians in Corinth (16:12). When Paul wrote to Titus some years after the Corinthian correspondence, he said, "Make sure Apollos lacks for nothing" (see Titus 3:13). Apollos's reputation among the leaders of the first-century church was exemplary. He was spoken highly of, and as Luke says, "he greatly helped those who had believed through grace...for he powerfully refuted the Jews in public, demonstrating by the Scriptures that Jesus was the Christ" (Acts 18:27-28).

May the things that were said of Apollos by Luke be said of you as well. Something will be thought of you, said of you, inscribed of you on your tombstone. May others say that you were an eloquent man, competent in the Scriptures, instructed in the way the Lord, and fervent in spirit. May you be known for speaking and teaching accurately the things concerning Jesus, and for speaking these things boldly.

PRAYER

Father, we thank You for this text. Make us humble in spirit such that we accept the correction of those who are friends to the gospel. And may our congregations bear the marks of a church that would produce an Apollos and be filled with Priscillas and Aquilas, and may all the glory be Yours. We pray in the name of Jesus Christ our Lord, Amen.

A Tale of Two Preachers

"Pilate said to them, 'Then what shall I do
with Jesus, who is called Christ?'"

Matthew 27:22

12

A Tale of Two Preachers

John MacArthur
Shepherds' Conference 2013

Matthew 26–27

Through all the years of my ministry, I have been concerned by a disturbing reality—the fact that the church is occupied by people who aren't really saved. I have written many books on this subject, including *The Gospel According to Jesus, The Gospel According to the Apostles, Ashamed of the Gospel, The Truth War,* and *Hard to Believe.* These books highlight that the church is full of people who are on their way to hell. If we are to throw our bodies in front of perishing sinners, then we have to start in the church. We can't make assumptions.

In the mid-twentieth century, there were two young and gifted evangelists. They came onto the scene in the United States at the same time. They were called the "Gold Dust Twins."[1] One of those two young evangelists you know very well, Billy Graham. His story is common knowledge and as of this writing is still being lived out. The other young evangelist was Charles Templeton, whom you probably don't know about.

It was Charles Templeton, Billy Graham, and Torrey Johnson who founded Youth for Christ. By all accounts, Charles Templeton was the more gifted preacher of the Gold Dust Twins. Intelligent, handsome, winsome, eloquent, oratorical, brilliant, persuasive, and effective—all those words were used to describe him. In fact, in 1946, the National Association of Evangelicals gave him an award—the "Best Used of God" award.

For a time, Charles Templeton overshadowed Billy Graham. He was considered a better and more effective speaker. The two of them went on an evangelistic tour of Europe. They preached in England, Scotland, Ireland, Sweden, and a few other places. They alternated as they went preaching to large audiences. Charles Templeton was given an opportunity to have weekly television programs on NBC and CBS in the 1950s. In the United States, he preached to as many as 20,000 people a night. He often preached in youth rallies with thousands of young people. He attended Princeton Seminary. He became a church planter, a pastor, and an evangelist with the Presbyterian Church. He even had opportunity to do a week of gospel preaching at Yale University. Charles Templeton was a formidable man.

But in 1957, Charles Templeton declared himself an agnostic. He rejected both the Bible and Jesus Christ. He attached the firmness of that rejection to reading Thomas Paine and other authors. He said that in ten days' time he read Voltaire, Bertrand Russell, Robert Ingersoll, David Hume, and Aldous Huxley. By the end of those ten days, he determined to leave the ministry. With $600 in his pocket, he returned to Canada and became a journalist. After being a journalist for a while, he became a politician, and almost became the prime minister of Canada. In 1957, he stepped into the eternal blackness of apostasy, blasphemed Christ, and signed off with a book, *Farewell to God*. So formidable!

Do you think there are other preachers like him? My dad was an evangelist. He ministered in Europe with another evangelist, preaching day after day, night after night in a very intense, prolonged series of evangelistic meetings. The other preacher was doing the same in another part of this great European city. When my dad came home, he said it was one the most horrible experiences of his life because this fellow evangelist was involved with drunkenness and prostitutes. How common a problem is this?

The guy who ran next to me in the backfield on our college football team, a co-captain, went to seminary and subsequently denied the faith. When I went to Talbot Seminary, I was friends with a young man whose father was the dean of the seminary. We graduated together. I launched into Christian ministry, and he ended up putting a Buddhist altar in his home. Over the years, I have witnessed ministers who remained faithful and ministers who rejected the faith.

The Two Preachers

I want to tell you another story, a tale of two preachers. These two you know very well. Both were called by Jesus personally. Both answered the call, forsook everything, and followed Him. Both declared repeatedly their personal devotion to Christ. Both were personally taught and trained by Jesus for preaching ministry. Both were intimately acquainted with Him every hour of the day, every day of the week, for years. They were taught by Him with perfect clarity, power, and conviction that had no parallel or ever will. They were taught by example and everything He ever taught them He lived to perfection. They were taught to know the will of God. They were taught the Word of God—to know it, believe it, live it, love it, and preach it.

Both saw the miracles of Jesus day after day as He banished illness from the land of Israel. No one has ever had a teacher who is equal, not even close. Both clearly saw the revelation of His divine nature. They saw His power over demons, disease, nature, and death. Both of them heard Jesus respond to every theological question perfectly. His answers always ended the discussion; there was never a need to say, "Could You clarify a little?" He answered profoundly, perfectly, and truthfully.

Both were confronted daily with the reality of their sin by living with the sinless one. Both were told day after day that every sinner needs salvation. Both were told about the reality of eternal heaven and eternal hell. Both received and used the very power the Lord Jesus delegated to them to preach effectively, to do healings, and to cast out demons. Both exercised that power and both preached Jesus as Messiah, Savior, Son of Man, and Son of God.

They shared all of this together. They were exposed to Jesus in identical ways. And there's more: Both were sinners, and they knew it. Both were so aware of their sin that they were overwhelmed with guilt to a crushing level. Both gave themselves over to Satan and took up Satan's cause. In the end, both of them betrayed Jesus boldly, emphatically, openly, publicly, and resolutely. They both did this at the end of all their training and experience. Just before Jesus was crucified, both of them were completely devastated by what they had done.

One of them, in spite of his wicked betrayal of the Savior, is considered so honorable, so noble, and such a grand figure that millions of people have been named after him—Peter. There's even a feminine form of his name across the world, *Petra*. The other man...not so much. He is considered so dishonorable and so despicable that although his name means "praised," very few people have it. His name is hated and reviled by many.

One of those preachers ended his life a suicide, hanging himself, and being eternally banished. The other ended his life a saint, crucified upside down, but eternally blessed. One of them we will meet in heaven. The other one will be met in hell by those who reject Christ. You'd have to go to hell to meet Judas and other apostate and defecting preachers.

**The bottom line for every person is this:
What do you think of Christ?**

Two men, side by side with each other and with Jesus for three years, and then separated from each other for all eternity. One of them is the first name in each of the four New Testament lists of the apostles. The other one is the last name in every list. One of them is enthroned in highest heaven, and the other one is consigned to lowest hell. One of them will be honored forever, and the other will be tortured forever. Amazingly, both betrayed the Lord Jesus, and both regretted what they had done; both were sorry. All this brings us to an important point: Salvation can't be by works because they both did the same works; they both did miracles. Salvation can't be by knowledge; they both had the same information. So what was the difference between the two?

What Do You Think of Christ?

Let me tell you what the difference was. It's important for you to know because every minister should make it a high priority to be sure that the people in his church are genuinely saved. What accounted for the difference? Their attitudes toward the Lord Jesus. The bottom line for every person is this: What do you think of Christ? That's what explains the difference between Peter and Judas, and we need to be aware of that when it comes to the people in our churches today. Every church is full of Peters and Judases. They are full of people hearing the same messages, experiencing the same worship, and seeing the same power on display in people's lives, but they're going to end up in two extremely different destinations.

Isn't that what Jesus said would happen? At the end of the Sermon on the Mount, He said, "Many will say to Me on that day, 'Lord, Lord.'" And to a large number of them He will respond, "I never knew you" (Matthew 7:21-23). It all comes back to one's attitude toward Jesus Christ.

Through the years, people have asked me, "Why are you so stuck on preaching Christ?" It's because I know that what saves people from hell is a right attitude toward Jesus Christ. I can't preach enough of Him. That's the point of all of Scripture—to point to Him. I make no apology for following my mentor, the apostle Paul, who preached Christ and was determined "to know nothing among you except Jesus Christ, and Him crucified" (1 Corinthians 2:2).

Setting the Stage

To see these two preachers in action, let's look together at Matthew 26. Matthew opened the chapter with "When Jesus finished all these words…" That is, Jesus had just given the great Olivet Discourse, the sermon on His second coming. Then He said, "You know that after two days the Passover is coming, and the Son of Man is to be handed over for crucifixion" (verse 2). He had told this to the Twelve before—back in Matthew 16:21, we read, "From that time Jesus began to show His disciples that He must go to Jerusalem and suffer many things from the elders and chief priests and scribes, and be killed, and be raised up on the third day."

This was too much for Peter to swallow. "Peter took Him aside and began to rebuke Him, saying, 'God forbid it, Lord! This shall never happen to You.' But He turned and said to Peter, 'Get behind me, Satan!'" (verses 22-23). Jesus repeatedly told the disciples that He was going to die, and He even gave them details about what would happen—how He would be treated, who was going to do it, and that the plan was in motion.

Going back to Matthew 26, in verse 3 we read, "Then the chief priests and the elders of the people were gathered together in the court of the high priest, named Caiaphas; and they plotted together to seize Jesus by stealth and kill Him." That was the plan—capture and kill Jesus. In the meantime, Jesus was in Bethany, at the home of Simon the leper. While He was there, "a woman came to Him with an alabaster vial of very costly perfume, and she poured it on His head as He reclined at the table. But the disciples were indignant when they saw this, and said, 'Why this waste? For this perfume might have been sold for a high price and the money given to the poor" (Matthew 26:7-9). Though we are told the disciples said this, John 12:4 more specifically reports it was Judas who said it. He was the protestor.

Judas, a Master Hypocrite

Here is the first time in the Gospel record that Judas reveals his inner character. Up to this point, we know quite a bit about Peter, James, and John, but we don't have much information about Judas. There was no reason to suspect anything was amiss. Judas didn't seem to respond any differently than the rest of the Twelve to what Jesus said or did. There was no suspicion regarding Judas's character, but here in Matthew 26 Judas questions a woman's use of expensive perfume, making it evident he wanted the money that could have been obtained by selling the perfume.

In His rebuke to the disciples, Jesus said, "When she poured this perfume on my body, she did it to prepare me for burial" (Matthew 26:12). But Judas wasn't thinking about that. He had his own agenda—he wanted money, power, and prestige. He wanted to be in the power seat when Jesus set up His kingdom, and his ambitions were being smashed by all this talk of crucifixion, death, and burial. This was massively disappointing to Judas.

Look at what happened next: "Then one of the twelve, named Judas Iscariot, went to the chief priests and said, 'What are you willing to give me to betray Him to you?' And they weighed out thirty pieces of silver to him. From then on he began looking for a good opportunity to betray Jesus" (verses 14-16). Judas went to the chief priests, and they weighed out 30 pieces of silver. This, according to Exodus 21:32, was the price of a slave. This is just shocking—Judas, who had been trusted with a great stewardship along with the other disciples, was going to betray the Son of God for the price of a slave.

We continue in verses 17-19: "Now on the first day of Unleavened Bread the disciples came to Jesus and asked, 'Where do You want us to prepare for You to eat the Passover?' And He said, 'Go into the city to a certain man, and say to him, "The Teacher says, my time is near; I am to keep the Passover at your house with My disciples."' The disciples did as Jesus had directed them; and they prepared the Passover." The Passover was established back in Exodus 12, and they were going to observe this annual event together.

You know the rest of the story: "Now when evening came, Jesus was reclining at the table with the twelve disciples. As they were eating, He said, 'Truly I say to you that one of you will betray me.'" This came as a total shock to the group. "Being deeply grieved, they each one began to say to Him, 'Surely not I, Lord.'" Notice the disciples suspected themselves before they suspected anyone else, including Judas. Nothing had happened yet that would cause them to look at him.

Then Jesus said, "He who dipped his hand with Me in the bowl is the one who will betray Me" (verse 23). During the Passover supper, they ate their meal using a communal bowl into which they could dip their bread. Jesus continued, "'The Son of Man is to go, just as it is written of Him; but woe to the man by whom the Son of Man is betrayed! It would have been good for that man if he had not been born.' And Judas, who was betraying Him, said, 'Surely it is not I, Rabbi?' Jesus said to him, 'You have said it yourself'" (verses 24-25).

Judas had already made the deal, and now he was waiting for the opportune moment to betray Jesus. This may be one of the most horrendous moments in human history. Nobody suspected Judas, and he thought he could get away with another statement of hypocrisy. He was a master of hypocrisy.

The Betrayal

After the Passover meal, Jesus departed with the disciples for the Garden of Gethsemane. We are told that "after singing a hymn, they went out to the Mount of Olives" (verse 30). When they arrived at the garden, Jesus said to His disciples, "Sit here while I go over there and pray" (verse 36). Then He went a bit further with Peter and the two sons of Zebedee, asking them to keep watch and pray. But the three disciples could not stay awake and ended up falling asleep. When Jesus returned, "He came to the disciples and said to them, 'Are you still sleeping and resting? Behold, the hour is at hand and the Son of Man is being betrayed into the hands of sinners. Get up, let us be going; behold, the one who betrays Me is at hand!'" (verses 45-46).

Judas goes into action, and as he does, we are reminded in verse 47 that he was "one of the twelve." Every time Judas and the betrayal are mentioned together in the Gospels, the passage always identifies him as one of the Twelve. This underscores just how shocking and inconceivable his betrayal was.

John informs us that it was at this point that Satan entered Judas (John 13:27). Jesus was never fooled. He knew all along that Judas was the son of perdition. In fact, in John 6:70, Jesus said, "Did I Myself not choose you, the twelve, and yet one of you is a devil?"

So Jesus was in the garden, and Judas showed up with a massive entourage that included the chief priests, the elders, the temple police with their clubs and swords, and no doubt some of the Romans. They were all coming to arrest Him.

Verse 48 continues, "Now he who was betraying Him gave them a sign, saying, 'Whomever I kiss, He is the one; seize Him.' Immediately Judas went to Jesus and said, 'Hail, Rabbi!' and kissed Him." Jesus responded by addressing Judas as "friend" (verse 50). In the original Greek text, this is not the usual word for friend. Instead, Jesus used a word that speaks of an associate—it is more technical than personal, as if He were saying, "Associate, do what you have come for." Then the people "came and laid hands on Jesus and seized Him" (verse 50).

Matthew 26:57-60 tells what happened next:

> Those who had seized Jesus led Him away to Caiaphas, the high priest, where the scribes and elders were gathered together. But Peter was following Him at a distance as far as the courtyard of the high priest, and entered in, and sat down with the officers to see the outcome. Now the chief priests and the whole Council kept trying to obtain false testimony against Jesus, so that they might put Him to death. They did not find any, even though many false witnesses came forward.

What was the outcome of the trial? Verse 65 says that "the high priest tore his robes and said, 'He has blasphemed! What further need do we have of witnesses?'" They were outraged by Jesus' comments and declared that He deserved death. So they began to mistreat Jesus: "They spat on His face and beat Him with their fists; and others slapped Him, and said, 'Prophesy to us, You Christ; who is the one who hit You?'" (verses 67-68). Matthew 27 opens with the following scene:

> Now when morning came, all the chief priests and the elders of the people conferred together against Jesus to put Him to death; and they bound Him, and led Him away and delivered Him to Pilate the governor.

> Then when Judas, who had betrayed Him, saw that He had been condemned, he felt remorse and returned the thirty pieces of silver to the chief priest and elders, saying, "I have sinned by betraying innocent blood." But they said, "What is that to us? See to that yourself." And he threw the pieces of silver into the temple sanctuary and departed; and he went away and hanged himself. The chief priests took the pieces of silver and said, "It is not lawful to put them into temple treasury, since it is the price of blood." And they conferred together and with the money bought the Potter's Field as a burial place for strangers.

> For this reason that field has been called the Field of Blood to this day. Then that which was spoken through Jeremiah the

prophet was fulfilled: "And they took the thirty pieces of silver, the price of the one whose price had been set by the sons of Israel; and they gave them for the Potter's Field, as the Lord directed me" (verses 1-10).

It wasn't lawful for the chief priests and the elders to do what they had done to Jesus, but that didn't bother them. Now, you may wonder why this passage identifies Jeremiah as the source of the Old Testament quote. It's actually Zechariah, but the reason Jeremiah is identified is because the Old Testament is divided into three sections. You have the Law, the Writings, and the Prophets. Jeremiah was the first book of the Prophets in the Hebrew text, and so Jeremiah became the title for that section.

The historical account continues as we see the horrible tragedy of Judas unfold. He hung himself. Acts 1:18 says he died by "falling headlong…and all his intestines gushed out." Evidently when he hung himself, either the rope or branch broke and his body was dashed against the ground. What a horrible and unparalleled tragedy. In fact, this is the greatest tragedy in human history because Judas had unequalled opportunity to see Jesus up close.

Yet Judas remained greedy, materialistic, earthly, and motivated by personal ambition. His desire for riches was so great that he ignored the truth that was in his face. Judas went to hell on purpose. He knew there was a hell, and he made the choice to send himself there. It's as if he said, "The agony is too great. I want relief. I'm going to send myself to hell." His downfall came because he loved himself too much, he rejected salvation too easily, and he resented Jesus too strongly. The same sun that melts the wax hardens the clay.

Betrayed Again

Next we direct our focus to Peter. Going back to Matthew 26:17-19, we read,

> Now on the first day of the Unleavened Bread the disciples came to Jesus and asked, "Where do You want us to prepare for You to eat the Passover?" and He said, "Go into the city to a certain man, and say to him, 'The Teacher says, "My time is

near, I am to keep the Passover at your house with My disciples.""" The disciples did as Jesus had directed them; and they prepared the Passover.

Jesus planned the Passover in such a way that Judas didn't know where it was going to take place. This meant he couldn't lead people there to arrest Jesus.

Verse 26 continues, "While they were eating, Jesus took some bread, and after a blessing, He broke it and gave it to the disciples, and said, 'Take, eat; this is my body.'" And with these words Jesus transitions the Passover into the Lord's Supper. Then after they sang a hymn they went to the Mount of Olives. As they did so, Jesus said, "You will all fall away because of Me this night, for it is written, 'I will strike down the shepherd, and the sheep of the flock shall be scattered.' But after I have been raised, I will go ahead of you to Galilee." But Peter said to Him, 'Even though all may fall away because of You, I will never fall away'" (26:31-33).

Jesus told the Twelve they would all defect, but Peter thought more highly of himself than he should have. Jesus responded, "Truly I say to you that this very night, before a rooster crows, you will deny me three times" (verse 34). Peter protested, "'Even if I have to die with You, I will not deny You.' All the disciples said the same thing too" (verse 35).

But as we well know, Peter went on to deny Christ. His crime was as evil, resolute, and public as Judas's. He wouldn't know it, however, until the rooster crowed.

Let's look at what happened: "Now Peter was sitting outside in the courtyard, and a servant-girl came to him and said, 'You too were with Jesus the Galilean.' But he denied it before them all, saying, 'I do not know what you're talking about'" (verse 69). Peter then shuffled off to the entrance near the courtyard, where another servant girl saw him and said,

"This man was with Jesus of Nazareth." And again he denied it with an oath, "I do not know the man." A little later the bystanders came up and said to Peter, "Surely you too are one of them; for even the way you talk gives you away." Then he began to curse and swear, "I do not know the man!" (Matthew 26:71-74).

In the third encounter, when Peter "began to curse and swear," he pronounced a death curse on himself. He was saying, "If I'm lying, kill me." That's as bold as you can get, isn't it? Peter's denial was blatant.

Right after Peter's outburst, "immediately a rooster crowed" (verse 74). In that instant, Peter remembered Jesus' words: "Before a rooster crows, you will deny Me three times" (verse 34). He had pronounced a death sentence on himself—"Take my life if I'm lying"—even though he had already lied.

What did Peter do? Did he hang himself? No, he went out and wept bitterly. Luke provides an amazing detail here for us. He says that when the rooster crowed, "The Lord turned and looked at Peter" (22:61). When Judas looked into Jesus' eyes in the garden, he kissed Jesus with the hatred of a hypocrite. When Peter looked into Jesus' eyes, he broke out in tears.

Crushing sadness without repentance led Judas to suicide. Crushing sadness with repentance led Peter to restoration.

How did Peter get to the place where he would end up denying Jesus? How could he do this after living beside Jesus for three years?

First, Peter boasted too much. Earlier, he told Jesus, "Even though all may fall away because of You, I will never fall away" (verse 33). In fact, he went so far as to say, "Even if I have to die with You, I will not deny You" (verse 35).

Second, Peter prayed too little. Remember what happened in the Garden of Gethsemane? Jesus came back to the disciples and found them asleep: "So, you men could not keep watch with me for one hour?" (verse 40).

Third, Peter acted too quickly. When the crowd arrived to arrest Jesus, "one of those who were with Jesus reached and drew out his sword, and struck the slave of the high priest and cut off his ear" (verse 51). This was Peter's doing. "Then Jesus said to him, 'Put your sword back into its place'" (verse 52).

Fourth, Peter followed too far. When Jesus was led away to the high priest, Peter tagged along from a distance. This led to the three encounters with people who accused him of being one of the Twelve—encounters in which Peter ended up denying Jesus (verses 69-74).

The Restoration

After the crucifixion and resurrection, Peter had gone back to fishing, which he wasn't supposed to do. He should have gone to Galilee and waited for Jesus to appear after they had met in the Upper Room after the resurrection. Jesus told the disciples to go to Galilee and wait. Instead, Peter had gone back to his boat and nets. He had returned to his old ways. Jesus showed up and confronted Peter, asking him three times, "Do you love me?"

What was Peter's attitude toward Jesus? It's very clear: "Yes, I love You. Yes, Lord. You know I love You." Notice that Peter even called on Jesus' omniscience. Why would he do that? Because it wasn't obvious that Peter loved Jesus: "You know I love You. You know everything. You know I love You."

The difference between Judas and Peter, then, was that Peter truly loved Christ. As the apostle Paul said, "If anyone does not love the Lord, he is to be accursed" (1 Corinthians 16:22). Later on, John wrote, "We love, because He first loved us" (1 John 4:19). Both Peter and Judas were present in the Upper Room when Jesus said, "He who has My commandments and keeps them is the one who loves Me; and he who loves Me will be loved by My Father, and I will love him and disclose Myself to him" (John 14:21). That night, Jesus talked to the Twelve about loving Him. But as it turned out, Judas hated Him—for dashing his ambitions.

In John 14:23-24, Jesus said, "If anyone loves Me, he will keep My word; and My Father will love him, and We will come to him and make Our abode with him. He who does not love Me does not keep My words; and the word which you hear is not Mine, but the Father's who sent me." It's all about loving Christ. As Jesus said in John 14:28, "You heard that I said to you, 'I go away, and I will come to you.' If you loved Me, you would have rejoiced because I go the Father, for the Father is greater than I."

When Jesus spoke about His disciples' love for Him, He wasn't referring to some sort of emotional sentiment, some sort of buzz that He wanted them to experience. Note carefully how Jesus defined this love: "Whoever loves Me keeps My commandments." True love for Jesus responds to Him in disciplined acts of obedience.

The more you know about Christ, the more irresistible He becomes and the more you will love Him. Sadly, not everyone responds to Jesus the same way. In John 6, after a crowd of disciples heard some difficult teachings from Jesus, they walked away. Jesus then turned to the Twelve and said, "'You do not want to go away also, do you?' Simon Peter answered Him, 'Lord, to whom shall we go? You have the words of eternal life. We have believed and come to know that You are the Holy One of God'" (verses 66-68).

Peter had the potential for disastrous betrayal, but he was different than Judas because he loved Christ. For this reason, God went on to use Peter in powerful ways.

Captivated by Love

In light of the comparison between Judas and Peter, here's an important principle to remember: Sin and guilt do not produce true repentance. You can have powerful guilt, overwhelming remorse, agonizing regret, and still end up killing yourself. You can have an awareness of your sin and understand it fully, but that is not enough. Acknowledging your sin, feeling remorse over what you have done, and bearing the full temporal punishment for that crime doesn't necessarily produce repentance. The horror of Judas's sin did not make him repent. And the horror of Peter's sin did not make him repent.

The ugliness of sin is not enough to make the sinner repent. It can be enough to break you, to make you cry, to make you kill yourself, but it's not enough to make you repent. What is required to make you repent is a vision of Christ that elicits a captivating love. Peter loved Jesus. When their eyes met that night after the rooster crowed, Peter was crushed and driven to tears. His response was prompted by love. This reflects the mind of a true believer.

Peter later gave this testimony in his first epistle:

> Blessed be the God and Father of our Lord Jesus Christ, who according to His great mercy has caused us to be born again to a living hope through the resurrection of Jesus Christ from the dead, to obtain an inheritance which is imperishable and

undefiled and will not fade away, reserved in heaven for you, who are protected by the power of God through faith for a salvation ready to be revealed in the last time. In this you greatly rejoice, even though now for a little while, if necessary, you have been distressed by various trials, so that the proof of your faith, being more precious than gold which is perishable, even though tested by fire, may be found to result in praise and glory and honor at the revelation of Jesus Christ; and though you have not seen Him, you love Him (1 Peter 1:3-8).

When it comes to the people who attend your church, you are looking for genuine salvation. It shows up in a love for Christ that produces delight and obedience. Your responsibility, then, is to hold up Christ all the time—Christ, who is the most lovely, the most winsome, the most beautiful, the most glorious, the most magnificent, and the most perfect One of all. You can't offer people anything better.

There is tremendous joy in having a congregation that loves Christ, because that love compels the people to honor and serve Him.

Giving People a Hunger for Christ

After I finished preaching through the entire New Testament I asked the people in my church, "Well, what do you want now?" They said, "Show us Christ in the Old Testament." I went to the Old Testament and for months, we learned about the pre-incarnate Christ. Then I said, "What now?" The church said, "Preach through the Gospel of John *again*." So we went back to the Gospel of John. Why? Believers want to see Christ. It's His beauty that overwhelms them. He's the one they love. Like Peter, they love Christ.

There is tremendous joy in having a congregation that loves Christ, because that love compels the people to honor and serve Him. So don't give your congregation some emotional, sentimental buzz. As a preacher, it is your duty and privilege to show them Christ.

That concludes our tale of two preachers. Until the end, Judas and Peter were indistinguishable to their close friends. But as it turned out, Judas belonged to Satan, and Peter belonged to the Savior.

Last Words

Charles Templeton died in 2001 at the age of 86. We have only one quote from him as he was dying. He said of Jesus, "I miss Him."[2] I think that's what Judas will say forever as well: "I miss Jesus."

You don't need to miss Jesus. You can be in His presence forever. Don't be a defecting preacher. Hold up Jesus for your people so they can love Him like you love Him.

PRAYER

Father, we thank You for the beauty, power, and clarity of Scripture. We are so blessed. This Book is overwhelming in its power. Thank You for the tale of two preachers that You've reminded us of once again. One day, we want to gather with all those preachers who are around Peter. May no one in this place meet Judas; and may You help us to lift up Christ to our people so they can see the one to whom they can give all their love forever. We thank You. We love You. Though we don't love You as we should, help us to love You more. Amen.

NOTES

Chapter 1—Preach the Word (John MacArthur)

1. Martin Luther, as quoted in John Blanchard, comp., *Gathered Gold* (Welwyn, England: Evangelical Press, 1984), 238.

2. John Warwick Montgomery, *Damned Through the Church* (Minneapolis: Bethany Fellowship, 1970).

3. Marvin Richardson Vincent, *Word Studies in the New Testament*, vol. 4 (New York: Charles Scribner's Sons, 1887), 321.

4. Christopher Catherwood, *Five Evangelical Leaders* (Wheaton, IL: Harold Shaw, 1985), 170.

Chapter 2—The Call of God (Mark Dever)

1. Evan Esar, *20,000 Quips & Quotes* (Basking Ridge, NJ: Barnes & Noble, 1994), 224.

2. James Rankin Young, *History of Our War with Spain* (Chicago: Monroe Book Company, 1898), 73.

3. Clifton Fadiman and Andre Bernard, *Bartlett's Book of Anecdotes* (New York: Little, Brown, 2000), 465.

4. Henry Kissinger, *Diplomacy* (New York: Simon & Schuster, 1994).

5. James Gilchrist Lawson, *Deeper Experiences of Famous Christians* (Anderson, IN: The Warner Press, 1911), 303.

6. Jonathan Edwards, *Sinners in the Hands of an Angry God*, 1741.

7. Fadiman and Bernard, *Bartlett's Book of Anecdotes*, 160.

8. Jonathan Edwards, *The Justice of God in the Damnation of Sinners*, 1734.

9. Augustine, *Confessions*, X, 31.

Chapter 3—Epitaph of a Faithful Preacher (John MacArthur)

1. Napoleon Bonaparte, cited in Samuel Austin Allibone, *Great Authors of All Ages* (Philadelphia: J.B. Lippincott Company, 1889), 293.

2. Cited in Samuel Clement Fessenden, *Selections from the Speeches, Sermons, Addresses, Etc.* (New York: Wm. P. Tomlinson, 1869), 172.

3. Benjamin Franklin wrote this epitaph while he was still alive. It appears not on his original gravestone, but on a memorial plaque.

4. Robert Browning, "Incident of the French Camp," cited in Edmund Clarence Stedman, ed., *A Victorian Anthology, 1837-1895*, vol. 2 (Cambridge: Riverside Press, 1895), 346.

5. Rudyard Kipling, *The Works of Rudyard Kipling* (Hertfordshire, Great Britain: Wordsworth Editions Limited), 605-06.

Chapter 4—Bring the Book (Steven J. Lawson)

1. J.H. Merle D'Aubigne, *The Reformation in England*, ed. S.M. Houghton, vol. 1, reprint (Edinburgh: The Banner of Truth, 1972), 143.

2. Philip Schaff, "Modern Christianity: The German Reformation," in *History of the Christian Church*, vol. 6, 2nd edition (New York: Charles Scribner's Sons, 1901), 17.

3. James Montgomery Boice, *Whatever Happened to the Gospel of Grace?* (Wheaton, IL: Crossway, 2009), 83-84.

4. "Mr. Spurgeon as a Literary Man," in *The Autobiography of Charles H. Spurgeon, Compiled from His Letters, Diaries, and Records by His Wife and Private Secretary*, vol. 4, 1878–1892 (Cincinnati, OH: Curtis & Jennings, 1900), 268.

5. Martyn Lloyd-Jones, *Preaching and Preachers* (Grand Rapids: Zondervan, 1971), 24-25.

6. Martin Luther, as cited in *More Gathered Gold: A Treasury of Quotations for Christians*, comp. John Blanchard (Hertsfordshire, England: Evangelical Press, 1986), 243.

7. Phillips Brooks, *Lectures on Preaching* (New York: Dutton, 1877), 59.

8. John MacArthur, *Why One Way?* (Nashville: W Publishing Group, 2002), 34.

9. MacArthur, *Why One Way?*, 41-42.

10. Martin Luther, "On God's Sovereignty," in *Luther's Works*, 51:77.

Chapter 5—Preaching and the Sovereignty of God (R.C. Sproul)

1. D. James Kennedy, *Evangelism Explosion* (Wheaton, IL: Tyndale, 1977).

Chapter 6—Has Any People Heard the Voice of God Speaking…and Survived? (Albert Mohler Jr.)

1. Francis A. Schaeffer, *He Is There and He Is Not Silent* (Carol Stream, IL: Tyndale, 1972).

2. Carl F.H. Henry, *God, Revelation, and Authority*, 6 vols. (Wheaton, IL: Crossway, 1999).

Chapter 7—The Passion and Power of Apostolic Preaching (Steven J. Lawson)

1. Richard Baxter, as cited in Charles Bridges, *The Christian Ministry* (London: Banner of Truth, 1967), 318.

2. R.C. Sproul, *The Preacher and Preaching*, ed. Samuel T. Logan Jr. (Phillipsburg, NJ: Presbyterian & Reformed, 1986), 113.

3. Walter C. Kaiser, *Toward an Exegetical Theology* (Grand Rapids: Baker, 1981), 239.

4. Martyn Lloyd-Jones, *Preaching and Preachers* (Grand Rapids: Zondervan, 1972), 97.

5. John Calvin, *Acts*, The Crossway Classic Commentaries, eds. Alister McGrath and J.I. Packer (Wheaton, IL: Crossway, 1995), 33.

6. Iain H. Murray, *The Forgotten Spurgeon* (Edinburgh: Banner of Truth, 2009).

7. See at http://www.spurgeon.org/sermons/0027.html/. Accessed July 1, 2014.

8. Charles Spurgeon, "The Eternal Name," preached May 27, 1855 at Exeter Hall.

9. Richard Baxter, as cited in Lloyd-Jones, *Preaching & Preachers*, 100.

Chapter 8—Preaching in the Spirit's Power (Tom Pennington)

1. Meuser, Fred W., *Luther the Preacher* (Minneapolis: Augsburg Publishing House, 1983), 51.

2. Stephen Pogoloff, *Logos and Sophia: The Rhetorical Situation in 1 Corinthians* (Atlanta, GA: Scholars Press, 1992), Duane Litfin, *St. Paul's Theology of Proclamation* (Cambridge: Cambridge University Press, 1994), Michael Bullmore, *St. Paul's Theology of Rhetorical Style* (San Francisco: International Scholars Publications, 1995).

3. A. Duane Litfin, *St. Paul's Theology of Proclamation: 1 Corinthians 1–4 and Greco-Roman Rhetoric* (Cambridge: Cambridge University Press, 1994), 207-8.

4. Anthony C. Thiselton, *The First Epistle to the Corinthians* in The New International Greek Testament Commentary, eds. I. Howard Marshall and Donald A. Hagner (Grand Rapids: Eerdmans, 2000), 218.

5. John Stott, *Between Two Worlds: The Challenge of Preaching Today* (Grand Rapids: Eerdmans, 1994), 325.

6. Charles H. Spurgeon, *Christ Precious to Believers* (March 13, 1859), a sermon given at Music Hall, Royal Surrey Gardens.

7. D.A. Carson, *The Cross and Christian Ministry: An Exposition of Passages from 1 Corinthians* (Grand Rapids: Baker, 2004), 26.

8. Gordan D. Fee, *The First Epistle to the Corinthians* in The New International Commentary on the New Testament (Grand Rapids: Eerdmans, 1987), 94.

9. Litfin, *St. Paul's Theology of Proclamation*, 209.

10. Ewald M. Plass, *What Luther Says* (St. Louis, MO: Concordia Publishing House, 2006), 1131.

11. John Calvin, *Commentary on the Epistles of Paul the Apostle to the Corinthians* in Calvin's Commentaries, vol. 20, trans. Rev. John Pringle (Grand Rapids: Baker, 2003), 99.

12. Stott, *Between Two Worlds*, 320.

13. Stott, *Between Two Worlds*, 321.

14. Fee, *The First Epistle to the Corinthians*, 96.

Chapter 9—The Art of Crafting a Life-Changing Sermon (Rick Holland)

1. Harry Emerson Fosdick, "What Is the Matter with Preaching?" in Mike Graves, ed. *What's the Matter with Preaching Today?* (Louisville: Westminster John Knox Press, 2004), 9.

2. George Marsden, *The Salvation of Souls* (Wheaton, IL: Crossway, 2002), 11-12.

3. Jonathan Edwards, as cited in Marsden, *The Salvation of Souls*, 11-12.

4. John Piper, *The Supremacy of God in Preaching* (Grand Rapids: Baker, 2004), 57.

5. Alex Montoya, *Preaching with Passion* (Grand Rapids: Kregel, 2000), 151.

6. Jonathan Edwards, as cited in Marsden, *The Salvation of Souls*, 12.

Chapter 10—Preaching as a Dying Man to Dying Men (Alex Montoya)

1. For a more complete treatment on the subject of preaching, see Alex Montoya's book *Preaching with Passion* (Grand Rapids: Kregel Academic, 2007).

2. D. Martyn Lloyd-Jones, *Preaching & Preachers* (Grand Rapids: Zondervan, 2011), 100.

3. Jerry Vines and Jim Shaddix, *Power in the Pulpit: How to Prepare and Deliver Expository Sermons* (Chicago: Moody Press, 1999), 347.

4. Lloyd-Jones, *Preaching & Preachers*, 93.

5. John Broadus, *On the Preparation and Delivery of Sermons* (New York: Harper & Row, 1944), 252-53.

6. Charles H. Spurgeon, *Lectures to My Students* (Grand Rapids: Zondervan, 1954), 307.

7. Lloyd-Jones, *Preaching & Preachers*, 87.

8. W.A. Criswell, *Criswell's Guidebook for Pastors* (Nashville: Broadman & Holman, 1980), 54.

9. David L. Larsen, *The Company of Preachers* (Grand Rapids: Kregel, 1998), 159.

10. Richard Baxter, *The Reformed Pastor* (Edinburg: Banner of Truth Trust, 1974), 61-63.

11. Robert Murray M'Cheyne, *The Works of Rev. Robert Murray McCheyne: Complete in One Volume* (New York: Robert Carter & Brothers, 1874), 211.

12. Lloyd-Jones, *Preaching & Preachers*, 92.

13. Lloyd-Jones, *Preaching & Preachers*, 83.

14. David Eby, *Power Preaching for Church Growth* (Fearn, UK: Mentor, 1996), 49.

15. Spurgeon, *Lectures to My Students*, 309.

Chapter 11—Apollos: An Authentic Minister of the Gospel (Albert Mohler Jr.)

1. See Ezekiel 18:13; 33:4.

2. Charles H. Spurgeon, *Lectures to My Students* (Peabody, MA: Hendrickson, 2011), 29-32.

3. As told in a 1943 UP news story, cited in Charles M. Province, *The Unknown Patton* (New York: Random House Value Publishing, 1988), 8-9.

4. John Piper and Wayne Grudem, *Recovering Biblical Manhood and Womanhood* (Wheaton, IL: Crossway, 1991).

Chapter 12—A Tale of Two Preachers (John MacArthur)

1. Marshall Frady, *Billy Graham: A Parable of American Righteousness* (New York: Simon & Schuster, 2006), 161.

2. Lee Strobel, *The Case for Faith: A Journalist Investigates the Toughest Objections to Christianity* (Grand Rapids: Zondervan, 2000), 18.

John MacArthur is pastor-teacher of Grace Community Church in Sun Valley, California, and president of The Master's College and Seminary.

Mark Dever is senior pastor of Capitol Hill Baptist Church in Washington, DC, and the president of 9Marks.

Steven J. Lawson is president of OnePassion Ministries and a professor of preaching at The Master's Seminary and at The Ligonier Academy.

R.C. Sproul is the founder and chairman of Ligonier Ministries and senior minister of preaching and teaching at Saint Andrew's in Sanford, Florida.

Albert Mohler Jr. is president of the Southern Baptist Theological Seminary in Louisville, Kentucky.

Tom Pennington is the pastor-teacher of Countryside Bible Church in Southlake, Texas.

Rick Holland is the senior pastor of Mission Road Bible Church in Prairie Village, Kansas.

Alex Montoya is the senior pastor at First Fundamental Bible Church in Whittier, California.

OTHER GREAT READING FROM HARVEST HOUSE PUBLISHERS

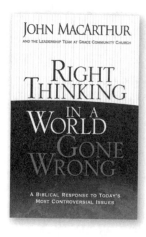

Right Thinking in a World Gone Wrong

John MacArthur and the Leadership Team at Grace Community Church

One of the greatest challenges facing Christians today is the powerful influence of secular thinking. This makes it difficult to know where to stand on today's most talked-about issues, including environmentalism, homosexual marriage, immigration, and the problem of evil. This book will arm you with right thinking and biblical answers to many of today's challenging questions.

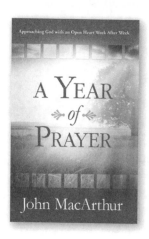

A Year of Prayer

John MacArthur

Each new day is yet another opportunity for you to draw near to God in prayer. He longs for you to enter His presence, pour out your heart, and trust in His care. But what to say? *A Year of Prayer* is filled with weekly inspiration to use as a springboard for your prayer life. Through these weekly prayers you'll find yourself lifted up...in true worship, praise, and thanksgiving.

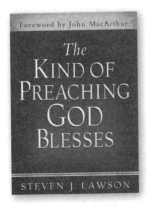

The Kind of Preaching God Blesses

Steven J. Lawson

Real power in preaching—that is, the power that brings true revival and transforms lives—comes from God alone. That is why it is so essential to follow the pattern for preaching given in Scripture—a pattern found in 1 Corinthians 2:1-9. Fulfill your high calling in ministry as you come to understand the priority of biblical preaching, the poverty of modern preaching, and the power of the Spirit in preaching.

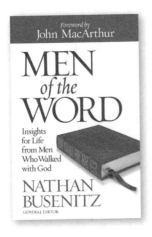

Men of the Word

Nathan Busenitz, General Editor

What is God's calling for men? What character qualities does He value? What is biblical manhood, and how is it cultivated? You'll find the answers to these all-important questions in the lives of the men of the Bible—men like Abraham, David, Nehemiah, and Paul. Every one of them struggled with the same issues men like you face today. From them you'll learn how to live by faith, lead with courage, pray with boldness, flee temptation, find satisfaction in God, and more.

To learn more about Harvest House books and
to read sample chapters, visit our website:

www.harvesthousepublishers.com

HARVEST HOUSE PUBLISHERS
EUGENE, OREGON